Advance Praise

"For fifty years the Korean Conflict has been the war that fell between the cracks; its veterans ignored and their sacrifices either overlooked or largely forgotten. In *Quiet Heroes* Frances Omori has done a masterful job of giving voice to one group of Korean veterans, the navy nurses. In their own words, these angels of mercy tell their story and unwittingly define what the word hero really means."

> Jan Herman
> Editor, *Navy Medicine* magazine
> Historian, Navy Bureau of Medicine and Surgery

"The human misery endured by many of the wounded during the Korean War can never be portrayed in words. Additionally hard to describe is the sense of having arrived in heaven when the wounded were finally attended to by the navy's angels of mercy. Comdr. Frances Omori's book, *Quiet Heroes,* helps marines say thank you to all the navy nurses, corpsmen and doctors."

> Col. Walt Ford, USMC (Ret)
> Editor, *Leatherneck*
> Magazine of Marines

"Were it not for the 'quiet heroes' who served aboard our hospital ships and at the Naval Hospital Yokosuka, Japan, there would be fewer of us to show them our appreciation on this, the fiftieth anniversary of the Korean War."

> Gen. Raymond G. Davis, USMC (Ret)
> Medal of Honor
> Assistant Commandant, 1971–1972
> Proud Member of the Chosin Few

"Frances Omori has carefully documented wonderful, true stories of real people that show the lasting power of goodness. This moving documentary paints a picture of selfless service—service that healed bodies and lifted spirits. Frances Omori has served her country well by telling the tales of these previously unsung heroes."

Vice Adm. Daniel Oliver, USN (Ret)
Chief of Naval Personnel, 1996–1999

"Though few in number, these navy women made a significant impact on the lives of thousands. Their professionalism, dedication, and compassion under grueling circumstances make them examples to be emulated. Recognition of these exceptional navy women is long overdue. The courage of these navy nurses is no longer forgotten."

Rear Adm. Henry C. McKinney, USN (Ret)
President and CEO, U.S. Navy Memorial Foundation

"At a time when we are losing our veterans and their stories at the rate of thousands a day, *Quiet Heroes* captures those memories and preserves a time in history for future generations to appreciate. Well done, commander!"

Sidney R. Slagter
Co-Author, *Chicken Soup for the Veteran's Soul*

"The tender loving care given to our marines by the corpsmen serving side-by-side with the marines in the foxholes and on the battlefields continued aboard the hospital ships and the various naval hospitals in Japan and the United States where the 'quiet heroes' performed their miracles. Those dedicated nurses applied their medical skills in combination with good cheer, optimism, and counsel—sometimes including admonitions—all to the benefit of the patients in their care."

Col. William Barber, USMC (Ret)
Medal of Honor

"A touching remembrance from a forgotten war."

James Webb
Former Secretary of the Navy
Author, *Fields of Fire* and *The Emperor's General*

"To the young marines they treated, the nurses were heroines in starched whites. They are remembered by the marines for their whispered words of caring, or a whiff of sachet and a calming touch through the miasma of pain amid the reek of battlefield muck and dried blood. But the 3,000 navy nurses who served during the Korean War were much more; they were caring professionals whose competence and skill in treating shattering wounds were instrumental in returning a majority of their wounded patients to the battlefield, surrendering only one-half of one percent. Comdr. Frances Omori has done America a service by writing this fine book honoring those unsung heroines of an unpopular and almost ignored war. Well done!"

> Frank Perkins, USAR (Ret)
> Military Affairs Columnist
> *The Fort Worth Star Telegram,* Fort Worth, Texas

"A great testament to the heroism of the naval nurses and U.S. Marines who served during the Korean War."

> Betty Ommerman
> Staff Writer
> *Newsday, The Long Island Newspaper,* Melville, New York

Quiet Heroes

Other books by Frances Omori

Strength Though Cooperation: Military Forces in the Asia-Pacific Region,
Institute for National Strategic Studies, National Defense University, (co-author).

Quiet Heroes:

Navy Nurses of the Korean War 1950–1953, Far East Command

FRANCES OMORI, COMMANDER, U.S. NAVY

Smith House Press

This book is available at a special discount for bulk purchases. For more information, please contact the publisher.

Smith House Press
2700 Rice Street
Saint Paul, MN 55113-2261
(651) 490-9408
FAX (651) 490-1450
E-mail: Smithseprs@aol.com

Library of Congress Cataloging-in-Publication Data

Omori, Frances,
    Quiet heroes: Navy nurses of the Korean War, Far East Command, 1950–53 / Frances Omori. St. Paul, Minn., Smith House Press, 2000.
        p. photos, cm.
    Includes bibliographic references, military chronologies and index.
    1. Korean War, 1950–1953—Personal narratives, American.   2. Korean War, 1950–1953—Medical care—United States.   3. United States—Navy—Nurses. I.   Title

DS921.6
951.9

LC # 00 131535

ISBN: 0-9615221-8-6

Project Credits

Cover Design:	Terri Kinne
Graphic Consultant:	Mary Firth
Editors:	Audrey DeLaMartre
	Amy Pavlis
Contributing Editor:	Dedire Samson
Proofreaders:	Robert DeLaMartre
	Amy Pavlis
Indexer:	Audrey DeLaMartre
Book Production:	Stanton Publication Services, Inc.
Book Design:	Donna Burch, Stanton Publication Services, Inc.
Publisher:	Sybil Smith

Printed in the United States of America

Dedicated to
Navy Nurses of the Korean War
1950–1953

For the names never remembered,
but actions never forgotten.

S. Sgt. Michael Maurphy, USMCR (Ret)

*If all that has been said by orators and poets since
the creation of the world were applied to the women of America,
it would not do the full justice for their conduct of the war. . . .
God bless the women of America.*

Abraham Lincoln

Table of Contents

Foreword

Courageous, professional, and undaunted in the face of danger, navy nurses of the Korean War heard the call of duty and answered unselfishly. They came from every corner of the nation and all walks of life. They joined the navy because they wanted to serve their country by sharing their professional nursing skills, by caring for those injured in body, mind, and spirit.

The navy nurses of the Korean War claim that they have done nothing special, that they were just doing their job. But in the hearts of all who served with them, the doctors and the corpsmen, and their patients, navy nurses of the Korean War are true American heroes.

Navy nurses came home from the war and for fifty years have lived as quietly as they served. Meanwhile, for those same fifty years U.S. Marines, their patients, have anguished that they were unable to thank these gracious ladies in white. For fifty years marines have held their stories in their hearts, remembering vividly their navy nurses, dressed in sparkling white uniforms, who were there for them in the darkest moments of the Korean War. They remembered pretty blue eyes, brown eyes, kind eyes, quiet voices, gentle hands, but the names were lost in the eternity of history.

For fifty years this nation hasn't known that this group of about 3,000 nurses volunteered to serve their country. They did it because they wanted to, because they cared about our nation. They wanted to share their nursing skills out of their respect for life.

It has taken fifty years for their collective story to be told. Through heartfelt personal stories, *Quiet Heroes: Navy Nurses of the Korean War* reveals the heroic actions and uncommon sacrifices the navy nurses made during the Korean War. These stories are told from the hearts and souls of the people who lived them. These stories are told because these heroes must be remembered, and because the actions of the navy nurses during the Korean War are what America is all about.

This book pays tribute to every navy nurse who served during the Korean War. Let us remember how these courageous, patriotic women answered the call of their country, and then came home to quiet lives, but lived on in the hearts of their fellow countrymen. Navy nurses of the Korean War, you are forgotten no more. You shall remain in the hearts and spirits of all Americans. Let your story be told. Let your story be heard. Let your story be preserved in our history and remembered for decades to come. Your sacrifices and uncommon valor sparks the fire of patriotism, the foundation of our nation.

Navy nurses of the Korean War . . . thank you from the bottom of our hearts. You are our heroes. You are *forever remembered* in the hearts and souls of your fellow countrymen. You are *forever remembered* in the history of our nation.

DANIEL K. INOUYE
UNITED STATES SENATOR

Foreword

World War II was over, and our nation had gone back to peacetime pursuits. Then abruptly, it seemed, the war in Korea broke out and our courageous young people were putting their lives on the line again. Among those young people included fighting marines and navy nurses, corpsmen and doctors who were brought together on the battlefield, in hospitals and aboard the hospital ships of the U.S. Navy.

The wounded marines were treated by gentle, attentive, selfless young nurses who had set aside their own lives to heal those who needed them. Some were recalled to duty and some volunteered, but they all came to give. And they gave unselfishly to patients who didn't know their names beyond an affectionate nickname.

I served with these men who fought. I know of their experiences in battle, and I have heard of their healers. Sometimes the men knew a first name or a nickname of their nurse, and often they voiced regret that they had never been able to thank them for their skill and kindness, compassion and dedication.

Now, with publication of *Quiet Heroes*, their grateful patients can thank those unsung heroes. This book honors the nurses and gives them the respect they earned so many years ago. Our heroes, all of them, will always be remembered with gratitude.

GEN. RAYMOND G. DAVIS, USMC (RET)
MEDAL OF HONOR RECIPIENT

Author's Introduction

"We're not veterans; we weren't near the front lines. We didn't do much. We were just doing our job. We're not the heroes; we weren't really near the fighting. We just did what we had to do, that's all."

Navy nurse of the Korean War, Marilyn Ewing Affleck, received an invitation to attend the opening ceremonies at the Korean War Memorial. She did not attend because she thought the invitation was for her late husband. These are the kinds of responses that come from women veterans most of the time. Women have never been drafted in the United States; they have always chosen to volunteer because they wanted to.

While researching information for a speech I was delivering at the Women's Memorial's first Memorial Day observance, I was intrigued by the letters I found at the Naval Historical Center, where women described "what they did during the war." But I was appalled that there was almost nothing on the Korean War women veterans.

I volunteered at the Women's Memorial to collect oral histories of female Korean War vets. Most who responded to the memorial's query thought their contribution, "if any," was insignificant. It wasn't until I attended a luau (Hawaiian party) that I met Marilyn Ewing Affleck, a navy nurse of the Korean War. Through her, a whole new world has opened up for me. A world I never knew existed. Each person I spoke to referred me to someone else. As the network grew, a beautiful story evolved. And to think that if it weren't for a luau, this story might not have been told at all.

Throughout history women have served our country and have fought in America's quest for freedom individually and in all branches of service: army, navy, Marine Corps and air force. They have become invaluable in the fields of communications, logistics, administration, and medical care. Army nurses worked in MASH units, air force nurses were stationed with air evacuation units and navy nurses served in navy hospitals and aboard ships. Some of their stories have been told. Only a few of these courageous, patriotic women have been recognized. To begin to widen this recognition, this book began as an oral history project for Women in Military Service for America (WIMSA). But then the need for a tighter focus was recognized.

During the Korean War there were about 3,000 navy nurses who served with uncommon valor at home and overseas. We focus here primarily on the navy nurses who served closest to the Korean front lines who were stationed on the hospital ships USS *Consolation*, USS *Repose*, and USS *Haven*, and at Naval Hospital Yokosuka, Japan.

For fifty years no one has heard of these nurses who worked so gallantly near the war zone. The nurses felt that they did nothing special; they were just doing their jobs. Yet, in the hearts and souls of their U.S. Marine patients, they were heroes. The U.S. Marines of the First Division have wanted to thank their nurses for many years, but they could not locate the nurses after the war because, in most cases, they didn't know their names. They carried in their memories the nurses' soft touches, kind smiles, warm eyes, gentle voices, caring attention, healing laughter, strong presence, and maybe a nickname. Somehow, names didn't seem to be the most important consideration at that time.

For fifty years this has haunted the men. So when the marines were asked to assist in telling the story of the navy nurses of the Korean War, there was an overwhelming response. One of the men contacted responded with:

> *Your letter made me sit alone in a dark room to cry for names never remembered, but actions never forgotten.*

Quiet Heroes is an account of the navy nurses who served during the Korean War told through personal observations from four points of view:

- their patients who remember them with gratitude,
- the corpsmen who worked with them,
- the nurses themselves,
- and the marines' memories, recounted from the depths of their hearts in words that bring tears to our eyes and a patriotic thrill to our hearts.

These stories describe quiet heroes and finally give them the recognition they earned. But also these stories serve to empower today's young women and bring pride to all female veterans who have served our country.

As I gathered this information, I made every attempt to use navy historical and official documents to preserve key historical dates and events. These documents, in the form of war diaries, command histories, and indoctrination manuals, served as the historical core of this book. But just as important, I made this a personal account with the stories gathered from the hearts and memories of the nurses, the hospital corpsmen, and the marines who were their patients at the Naval Hospital Yokosuka and aboard the hospital ships.

Since events are seen through individual perceptions, no two people will ever describe the same event in precisely the same way. Yet history's rich flow of events remain the same, only interpreted and personalized through the minds and emotions of individuals stationed in the Far East Command.

FRANCES OMORI, COMMANDER
UNITED STATES NAVY
APRIL, 2000

Acknowledgements

Many people have helped to make this diverse collection of facts, stories and pictures into a cohesive account of some amazing women. To those people I offer sincere thanks.

- Deidre Samson, who worked with me as an editor and ensured that my completed manuscript became a book in months, not years. She successfully led me to the right publisher. Without her expertise my book would not be a reality now.
- Alan Brudvig, owner, Falls Camera, and Chip Feise, photographer, spent countless hours and sleepless nights carefully scanning each photo and memorabilia provided by the nurses, corpsmen, and marines. They safeguarded each item and reproduced them in the highest quality to ensure that these fifty-year-old photos reflect the personal stories in the book.
- It took a caring, supportive community to help tell this story. Special thanks to all who supported and believed in this project: "My Gunny" Garrison Gigg and Carolyn Gigg who made the impossible happen; Gina Atkins, and Bernard Cavalcante of Operational Archives, Naval Historical Center, and his staff; Jan Herman, editor, *Navy Medicine,* and historian, Navy Bureau of Medicine and Surgery Archives; John Reilly, Ship's History Section, Naval Historical Center; Bob Aquilina, Marine Corps Museum; Phyllis Cassler, U.S. Army Van Noy Library, Ft. Belvoir; Rosemary Marlowe-Dziuk, National Defense Library, Ft. McNair; and the Department of the Navy Library.
- Many assisted with getting the word out. Thank you to: Col. Jerry Brown, USMC (Ret), chief administrative officer, First Marine Division Association, and editor, *Old Breed News;* Col. Walt Ford, USMC (Ret), editor, *Leatherneck Magazine*; Jaime Walker, *Leatherneck Magazine*; Scherlie Devine, editor, *Navy Nurse Corps Association News*; Tanya Ramey, editor, *Semper Fidelis Memorandum for Retired Marines*; Col. Robert Parrott, USMC (Ret), Chosin Few; and the Retired Officers' Association.
- My deep appreciation to all those who transcribed oral history tapes and provided on-call computer assistance and support: Joe Davis; Miyako Newell;

David "Kawika" Lee; Sharon Justice; Glenna Spencer; Nobel and Nora Nakagama. Thanks also to: Brig. Gen. William Weise, USMC (Ret); HMCS (FMF) Mark Hacala, USNR; Capt. Sue Miller, NC, USNR. From the Women's Memorial: Brig. Gen. Wilma Vaught, USAF (Ret); Judy Bellafaire; Britta Granrud; HMC Patricia Childers, USN (Ret); Linda Witt; and Marilla Cushman. Dr. Patrick Deleon; Bob Coleman; Mary Chatigny; Sherry Hayman; PH1 Daniel Taylor; PH3 Jessica McCahan; Rita Lara Bouchard and family; Ruth Hall, Korea Desk, U.S. Department of State; Col. James Hayes, U.S. Forces Korea; Comdr. Lee Jacobson, SC, USN (Ret); Mary Mulligan; and Verna Suit.

- I am truly grateful to editor Audrey DeLaMartre who believed in me and my book. She worked impossible hours, lovingly, and at lightning speed to meet impossible deadlines, and always with a smile.

- Of course, I am forever indebted to my publisher, Sybil Smith and Smith House Press for working miracles beyond belief to ensure that this book hit the shelves in time for the kick-off of the Fiftieth Anniversary of the Korean War. Smith House Press has truly defied all odds in the publishing world!

- And if it were not for each and every one of the navy nurses of the Korean War, their love of country, their professional nursing skills and the compassion they had for their patients, there would be no story. Thanks to the corpsmen, the doctors and especially the U.S. Marines, the patients, who shared their stories about these women. The response from the marines was overwhelming. They truly epitomize their motto, *Semper Fi*.

Because of the efforts of all these people who supported this project, navy nurses of the Korean War will be remembered forever.

Chronology of the Korean War

1950

25 June	North Korean Forces invade South Korea.
27 June	President Truman orders U.S. forces to support South Korean forces. UN Security Council calls on member nations for assistance.
1 July	First U.S. troops arrive in Korea.
16 August	USS *Consolation* (AH-15) diverted to Pusan while en route to Sasebo because of Korea's infiltration of North Korean Communists into the Pusan area.
17 August	*Consolation* is station hospital at Pusan to treat casualties from UN's fight against invading North Korean Army.
4 September	*Consolation,* underway for Osaka, Japan, diverted to Kobe.
10 September	*Consolation* arrives in Yokosuka, Japan. In dry dock until 13 September.
15 September	*Consolation* arrives in Inchon, Korea.
	Inchon Landings. Successful U.S. X Corps amphibious assault on Inchon. UN forces break out of Pusan and move toward 38th parallel.
	USS *Haven* (AH-12) is re-commissioned in Long Beach, California. Replaces the USS *Benevolence* that sank.
18 September	*Consolation* anchored in Inchon Harbor receives wounded from First Marine Division attacks on Inchon and Seoul.
20 September	USS *Repose* (AH-16) arrives in Pusan.
25 September	Seoul retaken by UN Forces.
2 October	*Haven* departs Pearl Harbor for Japan with twenty-five nurses on board, minimum required, thirty nurses.
7 October	U.S. ground forces cross 38th parallel.
9 October	Chinese forces begin infiltrating North Korea.
15 October	About 150,000 Chinese Communist Forces (CCF) cross Yalu River into North Korea.
18 October	*Haven* arrives in Inchon.
20 October	Pyongyang falls to UN forces.

25 October	*Haven* begins receiving patients from UN forces. During the next six-week period, daily average census, 530 patients.
27 October	*Consolation* arrives in Wonsan.
4 November	*Consolation* anchored at Wonsan completes evacuation of 64 patients.
13 November	*Repose* arrives Inchon.
19 November	*Haven's* high patient census of 778 leaves only eighteen empty beds. Repose departs Inchon.
20 November	*Repose* arrives Chinnampo.
23 November	*Consolation* en route to Hungnam.
25 November	Fifth and Seventh Marine Regiments reach Yudam-ni. First Marine Regiment deploys along MSR between Koto-ri and Hagaru-ri.
26 November	Eighth Army is pushed back from Yalu and retreats South.
27 November	Chosin (Changjin) Reservoir, CCF strike. Chinese launch assaults on leading elements of the Fifth and Seventh Marines for thirty miles down the MSR.
28 November	Members from 41 Independent Commando Royal Marines arrive at Koto-ri.
29 November	Task Force "Drysdale" moves north to reinforce Hagaru-ri. Column suffers 321 casualties, including sixty-one Royal Marines killed in action.
1 December	*Repose* departs Chinnampo with 752 casualties onboard.
2 December	*Consolation* at Hungnam with 648 patients onboard. Repose arrives at Inchon.
3 December	Pyongyang recaptured by CCF.
6 December	Fifth and Seventh Marines attack towards Koto-ri and the sea.
10 December	Lead elements of Fifth and Seventh Marines reach port at Hungnam. First Marine Division suffers 11,731 casualties.
24 December	Tenth Corps U.S. Army and 98,000 evacuate Hungnam and Wonsan.

1951

1–4 January	*Haven* at anchor in Inchon. Communists on the offensive reach the outskirts of Seoul in early January.
4 January	U.S./UN forces evacuate Seoul.
5 January	Seoul falls to Communist Army. *Repose* anchored in Inchon observes destruction of port facilities and supplies. Heavy explosions and raging fires all night. *Haven* is twelve miles from Inchon.

6 January	City of Inchon is fired upon and abandoned. *Haven* and three rocket ships the only remaining UN vessels moored in Inchon Harbor.
7 January	*Repose* and all UN vessels depart enemy-held port of Inchon.
8 January	*Haven* arrives in Pusan.
9 January	*Repose* arrives in Pusan.
15 January	*Consolation* arrives in Pusan
21 January	*Repose* departs Pusan with 301 casualties. Haven enroute to Sasebo.
2 February	*Consolation* in Pusan with 648 patients on board.
4 February	*Haven* receives urgent orders to Pusan to augment medical facilities of sister ship, *Consolation*. Casualties very heavy during the Communist offensive. About 700 patients are admitted during this time.
6 February	*Haven* arrives in Pusan. From 6 Feb to 13 Feb admits, discharges, or transfers 506 patients.
14 February	*Haven* departs Pusan en route to Inchon.
14 March	UN troops retake Seoul. *Repose* departs Pohang-Dong with 330 casualties. Arrives in Pusan.
26 April	*Haven* in Pusan. Communist offensive reaches terrific proportions and UN forces' casualties are high. Many very serious cases require immediate surgery. Surgical team works around the clock and the operating room staff is on twenty-four-hour shifts. Since patient load increasing rapidly, all patients requiring over thirty days of treatment are evacuated to Japan within forty-eight to ninety-six hours after admission to maintain empty bed space. As patient load becomes greater and total casualties remain comparably high, patients requiring treatment over fifteen days are evacuated to Japan. Haven in port 120 consecutive days.
27 April	*Repose* departs Pusan with 741 casualties.
8 April	*Repose* arrives Pusan.
5 June	*Haven's* patient load reaches 585; daily average 500.
13 June	UN forces retake North Korea capitol Pyongyang.
22 August	*Repose* arrives in Pusan.
7 October	*Repose* departs Pusan with 140 casualties.
9 October	*Repose* arrives in Yokosuka. Patients transferred to Naval Hospital Yokosuka because ship's water and sewer lines are clogged by jellyfish. Fresh water and high pressure used to blow out lines. Ship's crew and medical staff are granted leave.
22 October	*Repose* returns to Pusan.

1952

13 January	President and Mrs. Syngman Rhee of the Republic of Korea and U.S. Ambassador John B. Muccio visit Naval Hospital Yokosuka.
22 January	*Repose* departs Pusan to return to Long Beach.
12 February	*Repose* arrives in Long Beach for ship maintenance and installation of helicopter deck.
24 June	*Repose* receives first patient by helicopter.

1953

5 March	Soviet Premier Joseph Stalin dies of a stroke.
23 March	Battle of Pork Chop Hill begins.
27 July	Korean War ends as armistice signed at Panmunjom.

≋ 1 ≋

Navy Nurses of the Korean War

I was naked on my back on the bed. It was a genuine bed, with sheets, but I couldn't enjoy the luxury of it because the pain chewed at me. When I tried to lift my head, it pounded fiercely. I had just a glimpse of my feet. They were elevated and covered with white netting. I didn't know what was wrong with them, but they wiggled when I tried to move them.

"Hi, Marine." I looked up into the beautiful brown eyes of a navy nurse wearing a starched white uniform.

"Frostbite?" I asked. My raspy voice sounded like someone else. She nodded. This was the first I knew I had frostbite. Frostbite could mean amputation. That scared the hell out of me.

The navy nurse bent down beside me and held my hand. Her voice was soft, yet firm, "You'll be fine. It will all work out."

I was safe. I fell asleep.

2d Lt. Joseph R. Owen, USMC (Ret)

Navy nurses who served during the Korean War were the quiet heroes. They did their jobs and a hell of a lot more. They took continual care of routine tasks, yet responded immediately to life-threatening emergencies. They monitored temperature and blood pressure, cleared clogged airways, and responded to the injured going into shock. The navy nurses were always there for their patients.

Bloody, filthy, and in excruciating pain, the wounded arrived from muddy, frozen battlefields. Quickly getting patients settled and comfortable was foremost on the nurses' minds.

With the help of a corpsman she cut away the marine's uniform. She needed to know if there were any other injuries not immediately visible. She saw the bloody, dirt-encrusted bandages hurriedly applied days ago by a field medical unit. The corpsman removed the flak jacket. A shrapnel wound that had been covered by the jacket bled profusely. Nurse and corpsman exchanged a split-second glance.

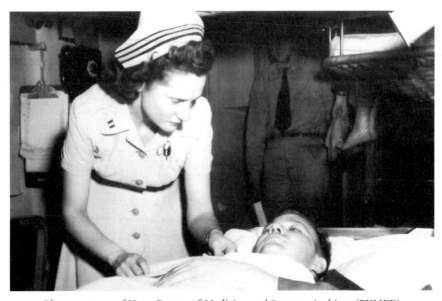

Photo courtesy of Navy Bureau of Medicine and Surgery Archives (BUMED)
Lt. Eveline Kittilson adjusting a sheet around a wounded marine who was just brought
aboard the USS *Repose* anchored in Korean waters.

They knew what to do. The corpsman scrambled for a doctor as the nurse applied a pressure bandage.

She looked into the dazed eyes of the marine. She held his hand. Her calm voice reassured him, "We've got to get you cleaned up first. Keep the faith. We'll take good care of you." The marine's lips trembled. He's just a boy, she thought. The doctor and corpsman were at her side. She heard someone three bunks away calling, "Nurse! Nurse!"

Navy nurses were in charge of a ward or wards depending on the size of the hospital or medical facility. The *Navy Nurses Guide* outlined her responsibilities succinctly.[1]

> *In the navy, the nurse finds herself in a unique position. She is appointed to care for the sick. She must be able and efficient . . . most conscientious in the performance of her accustomed nursing duties.*
>
> *In addition, she must be a teacher . . . clear-minded manager and a good leader. Upon her rests the responsibility . . . training and supervision of hospital corpsmen.*
>
> *In the shortest possible time, she must give her students satisfactory correlation between theory and practice. Corpsmen must learn the essentials of simple bedside nursing . . . special care of the critically ill . . . making of beds . . . habits of cleanliness and good order. We say, a navy nurse teaches as she serves![2]*

Photo courtesy of Agnes Sarna Renner

Ens. Agnes Sarna stands with her navy indoctrination class in San Diego, August 1949.

Photo courtesy of Navy Bureau of Medicine and Surgery Archives (BUMED)

Lt. Eveline Kittilson, discusses medication for the wounded aboard the *Repose* with a hospital corpsman.

And the navy nurses performed their duties quietly and professionally. Navy nurses of the Korean War were never truly recognized as heroes because their job description did not say "hero."

Having recently survived World War II, the American public was looking for heroes. Everyone loved a hero. Heroes had the high visibility, flashy, razzle-dazzle jobs. They churned and burned and flew thousands of sorties. They wreaked havoc and devastation upon the enemy. They drove ships into harm's way. They positioned crucial fighter aircraft. They carried vital fuel and supplies to the front lines. They hunkered down in foxholes waiting to charge the enemy. They marched as foot soldiers, facing the enemy squarely on the ground. They were the heroes! Heroes are admired and remembered forever.

Navy nurses were not considered to be heroes. But what they did was heroic. In the eyes of the corpsmen and doctors who served with them and their patients, they are true heroes.

When navy expectations of navy nurses were written, no one factored in the Korean War. No one anticipated the number of casualties. No one imagined the types of injuries the Korean War would bring. According to the navy, nurses would work in a sterile, well-managed environment. Their tasks, duties, and responsibilities were clearly outlined for them to follow. Hospitals were orderly, efficient, and organized. Nurses were taught to "go by the book."

According to "the book," every week on Friday, commencing at 1000 (10:00 AM), the commanding officer of the hospital inspected each ward. This was to ensure command readiness. To prepare, everything was removed from patients' lockers, the lockers were cleaned thoroughly inside and out, and clothing was returned to the locker, neatly folded. The corpsmen ensured that patients did not keep food, dishes, or unnecessary items in the footlocker. If patients were too ill to clean their locker, someone was assigned to clean it for them.

Overbed tables were washed daily. The deck was swept and swabbed daily, and as necessary in between. Beds, examining rooms, diet kitchens, heads (restrooms), and doctors' offices were cleaned each morning. Each ward had a cleaning schedule to which corpsmen adhered.

Beds were lined up uniformly using the lines on the floorboards as guides. Each bed was two feet from the next bed. Freshly cleaned sheets were placed on the bed with tight hospital corners. Each pillowcase opening faced away from the door.[3]

A junior corpsman stood at the entry to the ward. As soon as he saw the commanding officer (CO) and the chief nurse approach the ward, he announced, "Attention on deck!" All eyes riveted on the door or entry into the

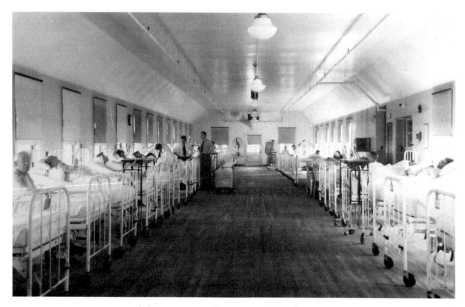

Photo courtesy of Virginia Jennings Watson
Ward 52 at St. Albans Naval Hospital in New York just prior to the start of the Korean War.

ward. The ward nurse and the senior corpsman met the Inspection Party at the entrance to the ward or in the hall. The Inspection Party consisted of the CO and the chief nurse. If the medical facility was small, there was a supervisor instead of a chief nurse. The ward nurse positioned herself to the left of the CO so she could furnish any information he required. The senior corpsman followed close behind the CO. The corpsman carried a flashlight, a bottle of rubbing alcohol and a towel.

A junior corpsman preceded the Inspection Party to open all doors. Each corpsman stood by his detail. These areas included the cast room or the dressing room where wounds were bandaged. All desk drawers were left partially opened. Charts and logs containing T.P.R. (body temperature, pulse, and respiration) and B.P. (blood pressure) were always up to date.

Charts had to be "accurate, legible. [They included] clinical notes and graphs . . . of value for diagnostic, teaching and legal purpose[s]." Charts were part of the permanent official medical records. The *Nurses' Guide* required that all official charts were written in blue-black ink.[4] If there was an error, the nurse had to draw a line though the mistake and write "error" on the line in ink. All errors as well as other entries in the clinical notes had to be initialed.

Ambulatory patients stood at attention. Those too ill to stand remained in bed, but they also were ready for inspection. The ward nurse and the senior corpsman remained with the Inspection Party. When the inspection was completed, they escorted the Inspection Party out of the ward. This was standard procedure, by the book.[5]

When the Korean War broke out, the system, "the book," went to hell overnight! A one hundred-bed hospital had to be converted to accommodate 5,000 patients. They stacked the patients on bunk beds, sometimes three tiers high. The wounded arrived in droves, in the middle of the night, by ship to ship transfer, by trains, helicopters, buses, ambulances, and boats. And they just kept coming.

Photo courtesy of Helen Brooks
Transferring patients from USS *Eugene A. Green* (DD-711), to USS *Consolation* (AH-15) while at sea.

Photo courtesy of Helen Brooks
Loading patients aboard the USS *Consolation* while in port at Pusan.
Litter hoists raised stretchers on board the ship.

Photo courtesy of Navy Bureau of Medicine and Surgery Archives (BUMED)
Injured being unloaded from HO5S helicopter on board the USS *Repose* (AH-16)
in Inchon Harbor, Korea.

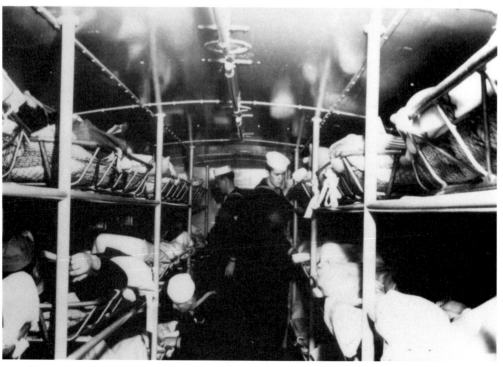

Photo courtesy of Navy Bureau of Medicine and Surgery Archives (BUMED)
Patients were transported by bus over bumpy war torn roads in Korea.

Photo courtesy of Helen Brooks
Patients were brought to the hospital ships by landing craft such as LSUs and LSMs.

On their battlefield the nurses witnessed vivid human inhumanity.

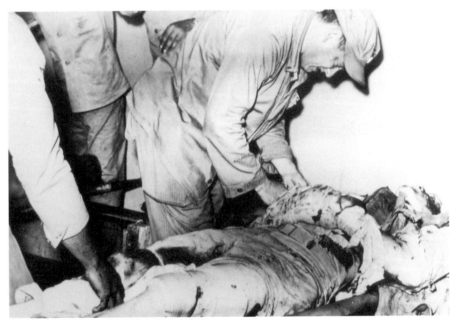

Photo courtesy of Navy Bureau of Medicine and Surgery Archives (BUMED)
Bunker Hill casualty, 18 September 1952. A physician cuts away the flak jacket
on a wounded marine.

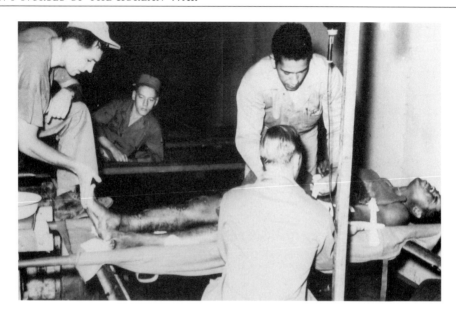

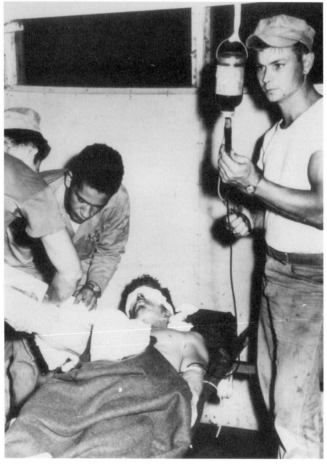

Photo courtesy of Navy Bureau of Medicine and Surgery Archives (BUMED)
Doctors and corpsmen care for patients from the First Division Marine at a forward aid station.

They looked into the frightened eyes of their patients. They saw unshaven faces streaked with mud, mucus, and dried blood mixed with grit and grime. They saw uniforms encrusted with blood and infested with lice. They smelled uniforms stained with stagnant water, urine, and diarrhea. They saw bodies encased in mud so dried and hard that they had to chisel and scrub the muck off. They saw feet so frostbitten that the skin was black and rotting away, exposing bone. They saw wounds treated and bandaged in the field, now oozing with pus and crawling with maggots. They saw mangled bones and skulls cracked open by shrapnel. They saw flesh hanging off the bones of soldiers who stepped on landmines.

They saw patients lined up stretcher after stretcher after stretcher. They heard the moaning, screaming, crying, cussing, and shrieking of the wounded who were packed into the crowded hospital passageways or put in warehouses until their disposition could be determined. Those suffering from combat fatigue were stashed under the stairwells because there was just no room.

Hospital corpsmen cleaned, scrubbed, and bathed patients at a furious pace, but there was always another trainload, another busload, another ambulance, another chopper. More patients and no room.

If anyone comprehended fully the human devastation and chaos of war, it was the navy nurses, the corpsmen, and the doctors. Although it sounds callous, these GIs on the front lines were regarded as military assets, and as such they were part of the U.S. fighting machine. Healing them was comparable to repairing an aircraft or a ship. Getting them back into the war zone was paramount to mission. This was the nurses' contribution to the war effort, their way to help preserve our national security. They got the fighting machines back to the front lines.

Navy nurses of the Korean War completed their mission, but from their perspective they were not returning killers to the front lines. What they saw were young kids like their brothers, cousins, and boys from the neighborhood back home. But they had a wartime mission, so like good sailors they held their heads high and completed their mission. They nursed the sick, and provided aid and comfort to the injured. They prepared the gravely injured for surgery. They assisted in surgery and were there during recovery. "We were nurses and did what was needed," said Lt. Marilyn Ewing (Affleck), Nurse Corps, U.S. Navy.[6]

To the hospital corpsmen, the doctors, and especially the marines who were their patients, it was obvious, the nurses went beyond the call of duty, beyond what was described as their assigned and collateral duties, beyond what was outlined in the *Navy Nurse Guide*. They performed unselfishly out of pride for their profession, they demonstrated loyalty to their country and love for their fellow humans. They rekindled faltering spirits, nurtured frightened young warriors, and salvaged what was left of human souls both overseas and on the home front. And many of these young women had barely reached adulthood themselves.

The Korean War hit hard and fast. Immediate deployment was achieved. A two-day turn around time from issuing orders to getting "butts on the bus" was common.

Comdr. Fred Smith, MSC, U.S. Navy (Ret), was a second class hospital corpsman when the Korean War broke out:

> I had just arrived at Norfolk, Virginia. I was at a place called Dam Neck when the war broke out in June 1950. We were watching the All Star Baseball game. A chief walked into the television room and said casually, "Keep on watching the game. Don't let me disturb you. Just wanted to say that the war just started. Some of you may be deploying on the hospital ship Consolation."
>
> And in two days, I was on the Consolation as she headed for Pusan, South Korea.

PO3 James Robert Standing was a corpsman stationed at Camp Pendleton:

> A few corpsmen lived in the marine barracks at Camp Pendleton. There were about thirty marines in our barracks. I remember a couple of nights after the Korean War broke out the gunny came in. He started calling out names. The gunny told the marines, if their names were called, they were leaving tonight. He told them to give any personal items to their buddies. They wouldn't be needing them because they were going to Korea. They had to be on the airstrip in two hours.
>
> Corpsmen serve with the marines in the field. I wondered when and which corpsmen would be heading to Korea.

By 30 June 1950, five days after the start of the war, 453 reserve nurses were on active duty. By the end of August 1950 the number had jumped to 800. The number of reserve nurses rose to over 1,000 for each month throughout the duration of the war.[7] They borrowed uniforms from their active duty counterparts to complete uniform requirements and were on their way immediately. Some were assigned to duty stations in the continental United States, while others were sent overseas to the Far East Command.

No war is compassionate towards military service members and their families, but the Korean War was one of the most disruptive. Many of the navy reserve nurses had served in World War II, and after the war ended they had just begun to attain some stability in their civilian lives. Some were now married, some had children, many were working in civilian hospitals and medical facilities. Although according to navy regulations married nurses were disqualified for duty, due to the rapid deployment no one checked changes in marital status of reserve navy nurses and all who were on the reserve rosters were issued orders and deployed immediately. That caused a sudden drain on civilian hospitals and medical facilities in the continental U.S.

By the time the navy discovered that some of their reserve nurses were married it was too late, because the nurses were en route to their duty stations or at overseas assignments already. These nurses had to be discharged and sent back home and, simultaneously, replacements needed to be found. Since there was such a critical shortage of nurses, the navy needed to keep the flow of nurses going to duty stations.

On 25 August 1950, the USS *Benevolence* was returning from sea trials carrying a complement of civilian and military crews. About two miles west of Seal Rock, in the thick fog off San Francisco Harbor, she collided with a civilian freighter and sank within half an hour. She carried fourteen nurses on board and was slated to be one of the hospital ships bound for Korea.

Then, on 19 September 1950, a military transport plane carrying eleven navy nurses headed for Naval Hospital Yokosuka, Japan, crashed in the Pacific. Replacements needed to be found immediately.[8]

Commander Fleet Activities, Yokosuka (CFAY) submitted a Historical Narrative to the Navy Department on 1 March 1951. As this report revealed, there was a critical need for nurses in Yokosuka in 1950:

> On 15 December 1949, the capacity of the Dispensary, Fleet Activities [Yokosuka] was reduced . . . from 250 beds to 100 beds . . . the allowance of Medical Department personnel was established:
>
> 6 Medical Officers
> 1 Medical Service Corps Officer
> 6 Nurse Corps Officers
> 2 Warrant Officers
> 44 enlisted Hospital Corpsmen
> . . . The patient load . . . for calendar year 1949 . . . was 78 [patients].
> The first Korean battle casualties were received by the Fleet Activities Medical Department on 18 August 1950 . . . and numbered 61.

. . . by 31 August 1950 the patient census had increased to 410 . . .
With the existing facilities and personnel, the patient load . . . had begun
to tax the department.

By 13 September 1950 when the Naval Hospital Yokosuka was officially established, the patient census was 492. The report continued with activities into November 1950:

During the period of 20 September to 30 September 1950, the patient
census . . . tripled thus resulting in considerable overcrowding.

The census steadily increased . . . 10 October 1950 [was] when the first
peak of 1,711 [patients] was reached.

On 30 November 1950, 1,402 patients were on the sick list. Of this
total, 544 were battle casualties. During the month, there were 796 ad-
missions and 268 evacuations.[9]

Yokosuka or Bust

Navy nurses began receiving orders to Naval Hospital Yokosuka. Lt. Marilyn Ewing was stationed at Camp Pendleton, working in the Dependents' Clinic, when the Korean War broke out. By July of 1950 she felt the tension rising at Camp Pendleton:

Each day, busloads of marines were being driven out the gates of Camp
Pendleton. All were destined for Korea. As the buses took off the
marines threw the last letters they had written out of the windows. We
picked up the letters and mailed them. We wondered how soon we would
be sent overseas.

Her premonition became reality in early December 1950:

It was a Friday and I was working in the delivery room. The Chief
Nurse's office called me at 1530 (3:30 PM) to inform me that I had
orders. I would be leaving for Naval Hospital Yokosuka, Japan, on
Monday.

Of course, I informed my family. They weren't too pleased that I was
going so far away. All I remember doing that weekend was getting my
shots and packing. It happened so fast. I didn't even have time to think
about the war and where I was headed.

Monday arrived and Ewing and (then) Ens. Betty Jo Alexander (Alex) and other medical personnel flew to Naval Base Coronado, then continued on commercial airlines to San Francisco. Delayed in San Francisco, they were to learn that this "hurry up and wait" was the way with the military. They traveled to Seattle, then on to Alaska. With each stop there were more delays, but only rarely were the delays explained. Their anxiety level rose as they headed "some place overseas" by unpredictable stops and starts. Ewing described what she was thinking:

In Alaska we were being held on the runway. We didn't know why we were being delayed. I guess a lot of us were still thinking about the military transport plane that crashed. The plane that was carrying eleven navy nurses bound for Naval Hospital Yokosuka. It crashed in the Pacific on 19 September 1950. All eleven nurses were killed. For some reason we thought we were going down also.

Little did we know at that time, that our plane was delayed in Alaska because it was being de-iced continually.

Courtesy of Marilyn Ewing Affleck

Ewing received her coveted IDLC showing proof of crossing the International Date Line.

Courtesy of Betty J. Alexander

Crossing the International Dateline at 0830 16 and 17 December 1950,
Ens. Betty J. Alexander had those traveling with her sign a dollar bill.

They finally arrived in Tokyo. Soon they would be on their way to their new duty station, they thought. Naval Hospital Yokosuka was about thirty-five to forty miles away. Wrong again. Another navy delay. This time Ewing was told why they had to wait at the airport:

> Trucks were sent to pick up the nurses at the airport. Somehow, someone thought we shouldn't be transported in a truck. So they sent for a bus. We had to wait another couple of hours for the bus to arrive.

Upon her arrival in Yokosuka, Japan, Ewing wrote on the first page of her photo album:

> My tour of duty starting 17 December 1950 . . . ending only God and Navy Department know when.

As an ensign, Virginia Miriam Jennings (Watson), Nurse Corps, U.S. Navy, received her officer indoctrination training (1948) at St. Albans Naval Hospital in New York. She worked and trained on the medical and surgical wards. In the fall of 1950 she received orders to Naval Hospital Yokosuka Japan:

> When I received my orders to Japan, I was elated. I knew there was a war going on. I wanted to do something for the war effort. I felt I was going to do something worthwhile. I was going to contribute my nursing skills. It was going to be wonderful!

Photo courtesy of Virginia Jennings Watson
Ens. Virginia Jennings, third from the left, and fellow nurses are about to begin
their journey to Yokosuka, Japan, 3 October 1950.

Jennings described her travel accommodations to Japan as "not luxury and endless":

> *We left New York aboard a United Airlines plane bound for San Francisco.*
> *It took forever, but we finally arrived in Guam where we stayed overnight.*
> *All I heard were those little lizards (ghekkos) climbing up the walls. The*
> *one thing that was going through my mind was I hope I never have to come*
> *back to this island.*

Photo courtesy of Virginia Jennings Watson
The front gate to 13 Halsey Road in Yokosuka, Japan. This was Jennings first "new home."

We landed in Japan in the early fall of 1950, just as the leaves were changing color. The nurses' quarters were beautiful. We were put into base homes.

Comdr. Lois Colgate Merritt, Nurse Corps, U.S. Navy (Ret), was an ensign stationed in Philadelphia when she received orders to Naval Hospital Yokosuka:

I got a call one cold night in Philadelphia from the Bureau of Medicine. They told me I would be leaving for Yokosuka, Japan, in a couple of days. They told me that Yokosuka already had 4,000 patients. We were desperately needed and had to be flown out very quickly.

Merritt also experienced delays: they flew from the East Coast to California, then stopped in Hawaii, Kwajalein, Johnston Island and Guam. Each time they stopped, it was for a few days. They were told that they had been pre-empted by soldiers going to the front lines:

By the time we arrived in Guam, we thought we'd be there for a few days. We hadn't seen our luggage since we left California. We were in the same clothes we had on when we left. By then it was kind of uncomfortable.

I happened to have a friend stationed in Guam. So I asked her to wash out our underwear. In those days they didn't have clothes dryers. Guam was very humid. But we felt we were going to be there for a couple of days, so it would dry before we left, but we left early the next morning and, when we put on our underwear, it was still pretty wet.

For Merritt and those with her, the adventure continued at Haneda Airport:

We arrived in Tokyo the night before Christmas 1950. Although slacks were not part of our official uniform at the time, they allowed us to wear slacks because of overseas travel.

As we walked into the airport terminal, we heard the announcement on the public address system that we couldn't go into the airport wearing slacks; we had to wear skirts. So where was our luggage?

Our luggage materialized. We had to scrounge to find our skirts, garter belts and hose. Then we had the challenge of changing in a very, very small Japanese ladies room.

Merritt finally arrived in Yokosuka wearing the required skirt:

Conditions were horrendous when we first got there. They stashed us in these little apartments, with twelve nurses in a three-bedroom apartment. We worked twelve-hour shifts. We were so tired. When we got off duty, we just wanted to go back to the apartment and crash.

Because the medical facilities at CFAY had to expand from a dispensary to a hospital overnight, navy personnel were displaced. The hospital needed their living quarters to convert into hospital wards. They were stuffing navy personnel anywhere they could find space.

No one ever imagined there would be this many people in Yokosuka at one time. They had to constantly keep switching our living quarters around. So when we came off our shift, we'd go back to the place we left in the morning, there'd be a note telling us where they moved our stuff . . . and where we had to sleep that night.

Photo courtesy of Lois Merritt
Ens. Lois Merritt, Ens. Nell Chumley (Long) and Ens. Bess Goehis on a stopover in
Hawaii en route to Naval Hospital Yokosuka, Japan.

One of the things Comdr. Florence E. Alwyn (Twyman), Nurse Corps, U.S. Navy (Ret), learned from the navy was flexibility:

> *I reported to Naval Hospital Yokosuka about two weeks before Christmas. I lived in quarters that had been dependent housing. Two or three of us slept in the dining room. We hung curtains to separate our "bedroom" from the "living room." Privacy was not an option.*

In November and December 1950, marines from the First Marine Division fought gallantly at Chosin Reservoir. They demonstrated, as marines do, their deep passion for their country. With temperatures dipping to thirty degrees below zero, the marines fought until they were too ill, severely injured, and too exhausted to fight any longer. Many were transported to medical aid stations. Some even came directly from the battlefield by helicopter to the USS *Consolation*. Others were transported by boats, trains, buses, and evacuation planes. They went to one of the three hospital ships and to Naval Hospital Yokosuka:

> *I was filthy dirty and sick as a dog. This navy nurse had me bathe . . . dump my filthy clothing . . . got me in a nice clean bunk with clean pajamas. She then gave me a tall cold glass of milk. She looked so beautiful in her spotless white uniform. I felt like I was home. I was safe. I fell asleep. I'll never forget her. Don't know her name. I never got to thank her.*[10]

This kind of sentiment was echoed over and over again by the U.S. Marines. They tell their stories about the navy nurses who were there for them, for all the thousands of marines, and United Nations soldiers.

It was Yokosuka or bust. The nurses overcame plane delays, endured unpleasant living conditions, traveled in wet underwear, and experienced days of uncomfortable travel. They went to a foreign place they never heard of. For the 200 navy nurses who served at Naval Hospital Yokosuka, their patients always came first.

Photo courtesy of Marilyn Ewing Affleck

Overall layout of U.S. Fleet Activities Yokosuka, Japan.

2

Yokosuka, The Hub of Activity

Commander Fleet Activities Yokosuka (CFAY) was the hub of activity during the Korean War and, steeped in a century of naval history, it became the perfect historical setting for their story. There were 200 navy nurses stationed there at the naval hospital, and it was there that the three hospital ships USS *Consolation*, USS *Haven* and USS *Repose*, came in for repair, to off-load patients, to replenish supplies and refuel. Then the navy nurses serving aboard, the ships' crews and medical staff came ashore for a well-deserved break, and the friendships made were nurtured so they have endured for fifty years.[11]

Photo courtesy of Lee Jacobson
Aerial view of Fleet Activities Yokosuka.

Yokosuka, a large sheltered harbor off the island of Honshu, provided an ideal location for what was once known as Japan's most progressive naval base. Established in 1884 by the Japanese, this naval base was known as the Father of the Japanese Navy, according to the Operational Archives Navy Historical Center (OANHC).[12]

On 27 September 1865, opening ceremonies were held for the steel mill situated on what was in 1871 renamed Yokosuka Shipyard. (OANHC) Tom Tompkins's book, *Yokosuka, Base of an Empire,* provides a detailed history of the base. In it he says that in 1894 they were constructing primarily small steam-powered warships at the shipyard. At that time Yokosuka Shipyard was credited for building the *Hashidate*, Japan's biggest battleship.

Other equally impressive ships were built, including battle ships *Mutsu*, *Yamato*, and *Musashi*, and *Hosho*, the world's first aircraft carrier, was completed in 1922. Twelve years later the first U.S. aircraft carrier, *Ranger*, was commissioned. By May 1933, Yokosuka Shipyard had completed building three out of four of Japan's four aircraft carriers. Finally, submarine tenders *Taigei*, *Shoho*, *Tsurugisaki*, and *Takasaki* were all built at Yokosuka.[13]

Employment

In 1925, there were over 10,000 men working in the shipyard. With the expansion of the Japanese navy, employment at the shipyard increased. By the end of World War II, there were 65,000 workers. After the Japanese surrendered, both Yokosuka Naval Base and Shipyard were turned over to the United States.[14]

On 30 August 1945, Rear Adm. Oscar C. Badger became the first Commander of Fleet Activities, Yokosuka (CFAY). The battleship USS *Missouri* was anchored in Tokyo Bay on 2 September 1945 and was the setting for the signing of the Japanese surrender documents.

Naval Hospital Yokosuka Established

The Kanto earthquake of 1 September 1923 leveled Yokosuka Naval Base and Shipyard. Most of the Yokosuka base hospital was destroyed and a makeshift tent hospital had to be erected to accommodate the injured. Reconstruction of the hospital, Building E, began in 1928, this time with reinforced concrete. It was completed in 1931.[15]

U.S. Naval Hospital Yokosuka was established in August 1950. On 11 September 1950 dedication ceremonies were held in front of the Administration Building at CFAY.[16]

Photo courtesy of Navy Bureau of Medicine and Surgery Archives (BUMED)

Front entrance to Naval Hospital Yokosuka.

Photo courtesy of Navy Bureau of Medicine and Surgery Archives (BUMED)

A bird's eye view of the hospital complex.

Naval Hospital Yokosuka's mission was to provide:

> *The treatment and care of sick and injured . . . naval and other United*
> *Nations personnel in the Far East Command. [This] include[d] the Korean*
> *battle area.*[17]

The main military objective for the hospital was quick turn around. That meant getting military personnel back to the battlefield. The hospital maintained and issued medical equipment and supplies to all units in the Far East Command, including the Korean battle zone. Also, in the event of a local disaster or emergency, the hospital was tasked to work with military and civilian authorities in matters of health and sanitation.

Before the United Nations Forces occupied Japan, the base had a sizeable Japanese medical center, including a large naval hospital. Due to the size of CFAY, the hospital was not totally in use when the U.S. took over the naval base:

> *At the time of the U.S. takeover, the average patient load for the dispen-*
> *sary was seventy-eight. By 15 December 1949, the 250-bed dispensary*
> *was reduced by the Secretary of the Navy to one hundred beds.*[18]

The reduction of beds resulted in reallocation of buildings assigned to the dispensary, and three buildings were converted into apartments. Those apartments, what had been four wards and quarters for 250 hospital corpsmen, became housing for twenty-one service personnel and their dependents.

Photo courtesy of Navy Bureau of Medicine and Surgery Archives (BUMED)
Entrance to what was U.S. Naval Dispensary Yokosuka.

Korean War Breaks Out; Hospital Expanded

When the Korean War broke out in June 1950, the dispensary consisted of nine major buildings housing:[19]

Operating rooms	Laboratory
X-ray	Physiotherapy
Diet kitchen	Dependents clinic
Dental clinic	Out-patient sick call
Pharmacy	Administrative offices
Quarters for service personnel	

According to a historical narrative written 1 March 1951, the navy had no idea of the volume of patients the war would bring:

> *The medical storeroom . . . contained . . . medical supplies considered adequate to provide medical care for 10,000 navy and Marine Corps personnel for approximately eighteen months. The equipment on hand would not have provided effective . . . care to more than 500 or 600 patients, and would have had to be augmented by additional new and modern equipment.*

The navy anticipated expanding facilities to meet the medical needs of military personnel in the Far East Command. In fact, the navy started to procure additional medical supplies, equipment, personnel, and infrastructure to treat up to 800 patients.

Reallocation of dependent housing was started in July 1950 to make buildings available for the care and treatment of patients of the Korean War. Patients included U.S., United Nations, and South Korean military personnel. Working twenty-four-hour shifts, Public Works remodeled and converted additional buildings to provide ward space. This was accomplished in record time, but due to the lack of living quarters, the process of relocating service members and families was slow.[20]

Lt. Comdr. Alberta Burke, chief nurse, expressed her concern for accommodating the ever-increasing patient census in a letter, dated 13 April 1951, to Capt. Winnie Gibson, director, Navy Nurse Corps:

> *[On] 10 October 1950, the [patient] census increased to 1,711 as compared with 492 patients on 23 September 1950. The period from 20 September 1950 to 30 September 1950 the patient census nearly tripled.*[21]

She described the process of expanding the hospital:

The recreation hall was converted to a ward. Double and triple deck bunks were set up in the hall proper, the stage, and the balcony.

Two buildings that were formerly part of a Japanese convent were used for wards. [These buildings] join the hospital. During a short period of inclement weather, it rained in through the windows and the roof leaked.

Photo courtesy of Navy Bureau of Medicine and Surgery Archives (BUMED)
Panoramic view of U.S. Naval Hospital and Receiving Barracks.

Mess Hall and Galley

Limited personnel, lack of supplies, ward space, and living quarters were just some of the problems. Food distribution was another challenge that was addressed in a report by Naval Hospital Yokosuka to CFAY, dated 1 March 1951:

The original mess hall for the dispensary was located in what is now Ward B. Food was brought from the station mess. The mess was located approximately half a mile away. Electrically heated food carts [were used] . . . to serve patients on wards . . . and . . . placed in the mess hall.

On 11 September 1950 food service commenced from Building E-17. [This is the] renovated galley and mess hall located on the hospital compound eliminat[ing] transportation of food from the main station mess.

The mess hall is a large "Quonset Hut" type building . . . commonly called "Elephant Hut" . . . with a seating capacity of 336. The maximum number of people served in this mess hall, at one meal, was 2,200. The maximum number of bed patients served at one meal was 1,800 . . . accomplished by the use of five food carts.[22]

In September 1950 plans were underway to remodel Building E-4-K, converting it to a mess hall and galley for an 800-bed hospital. By December equipment installation was completed and the special diet kitchen was transferred to the new mess hall. This freed up space in the dependents ward:

Japanese cooks, butchers and bakers were used to prepare food . . . supervised by navy cooks, butchers and bakers.

CFAY was responsible for providing fresh meat and vegetables to all U.S. and Allied ship and naval shore facilities. Food shipments from the States were not always reliable. CFAY began to use more local food supplies and in some cases the navy had to raise their own food. For example, when cooks and navy personnel complained about the strange taste of chickens raised locally, the navy raised their own flocks of chickens. They discovered that Japanese poultry producers fed their chicken fish byproducts, which caused strange tasting southern fried chicken.

Photo courtesy of Navy Bureau of Medicine and Surgery Archives (BUMED)
The "Elephant Hut" serves as the mess hall.

Housing

Hospital corpsmen were moved out of the four quonset huts, and officers were removed from their temporary Bachelor Officers' Quarters (BOQ) in Building E-9. Then Building E-6, acquired from the Sacred Heart Convent, and Barracks B of the Receiving Station were turned over to the hospital for emergency use and immediately they were filled to capacity.[23]

Japanese Nationals

By October 1950 there was a severe shortage of naval personnel. In June 1950 there were 8,410 Japanese civilian workers employed by CFAY.

This number was increased to more than 12,900 Japanese civilian men and women after October 1950. A few months later there were 16,000 Japanese civilians working at the shipyard, public works, and in the hospital complex where they were assigned to the mess halls, laundry, living quarters and hospital wards.

Patients Begin to Arrive

While the hospital renovation and expansion was still underway, patients from the Korean War begin to arrive. In August 1950, Pfc Herbert Richard Luster, USMC (Ret), arrived at Naval Hospital Yokosuka:

> *My right arm was amputated in the early hours of 18 August 1950 aboard the USS Consolation (AH-15). I was delivered by the AH-15 to Yokosuka Naval Hospital.*
>
> *Miss Marinack (spelling unknown) let me listen to her radio on low volume after lights out. I spent a lot of time talking to Miss Marinack. She was very patient with me. I often sat in her office late and talked to her.*
>
> *When no corpsmen were available at night, the nurses brought us a drink of water. Or they would contact a doc for permission to give pain pills. We amputees were stuck there for a long time. Having the nurses talk to us meant a lot.*

For the period 1 July 1950 through 31 October 1950, Naval Hospital Yokosuka admitted 3,895 patients, of which 3,160 were battle casualties. Naval Hospital Yokosuka was one of the main U.S. military hospitals in the Far East, and in addition to war casualties, the hospital still functioned as a military hospital. Dependents still had babies, got sick, injured and needed surgery.

The patient census tripled, overcrowding the hospital. Buildings located nearby, once part of the hospital, had been converted into dependent housing and now were being converted back into hospital spaces. Navy personnel and their dependents were on the waiting list to be moved to other quarters, but until housing was found for them, they could not be moved. That slowed down the hospital expansion project even more.

Photo courtesy of Navy Bureau of Medicine and Surgery Archives (BUMED)

Triple-decker beds await the arriving patients.

Photo courtesy of Navy Bureau of Medicine and Surgery Archives (BUMED)

With the massive influx of patients, regulation for distance between beds was dropped.

The unanticipated magnitude of medical casualties continued. In many cases beds were being assembled while patients were en route to the hospital and injured waited on the airfields for hospital beds.

On 13 September 1950 there were 492 patients at the hospital. Two days later 2d Lt. Robert F. Maiden, USMC, Platoon Leader, First Marines in Fox Company landed on Inchon, Korea. As his platoon moved toward Seoul across the Han River, he took shrapnel in his neck and left shoulder, shattering his jaw and cheekbone:

One of my navy corpsman gave me first aid. I was put on a jeep ambulance [and] taken back to Inchon. I spent the night in an old school house . . . being used as a first aid station. I spent the night there amidst the sounds of gunfire and bursting shells.

The next morning we were taken to the beach [to board] . . . the Consolation. There we received an evaluation of our wounds [and] given additional medical care. I recall a lady doctor who was in charge. She performed wonderfully as things were pretty hectic. I do not recall her name. She was a wonderful person and certainly was in charge.

Having survived thirty-four days on Iwo Jima four years earlier, I guess I thought I was one of the untouchables, but how wrong I was. After an insertion of a Penrose drain through my neck and lower jaw, they decided to wire my jaws. I had a broken mandible. I almost had my free speech taken from me [and] earned the nickname "Mumbles" from my ward mates.

A couple days later we were transferred to a landing craft. We sailed for Sasebo en route to Naval Hospital Yokosuka. We spent the first night at Sasebo in an army hospital. An army nurse tried her best to get me to turn in my personal jump boots. I registered strong objections.

Luckily, the next day we were put on a train and headed for Yokosuka USNH (U.S. Naval Hospital). I shall never forget navy nurse Ellie Hayes. She was one of the nurses on our SOQ [Sick Officers' Quarters] . . . a real gem of a person. She was a fine lady and an excellent nurse. She always went the extra mile to assist anyone in need. There were other nurses on our ward who were also outstanding. I cannot recall their names.

With my jaws wired shut, I had to make a daily trek to the diet kitchen . . . for my nourishment, which was all-liquid. This went on for thirty days till they removed the wires on my jaw. They learned I now had . . . ankylosis; I could not open my mouth nor chew normal foods.

Ellie came to the rescue with some snap clothespins [and] . . . taught me to exercise my jaws daily to overcome the condition.

Around Thanksgiving, I was flown to Oakland Naval Hospital for further treatment. It was now winter in Korea and being from Colorado, I knew all about winter. So I felt I had the better part of the bargain.

I kept Nurse Ellie's clothespins [and] made a satisfactory recovery . . . . So Nurse Ellie Hayes, if you are still out there, I have not forgotten the fine professional care you provided. You served so well and always with a smile or a joke or two.

Patient numbers increased to a total of 1,711 patients by 10 October 1950. The hospital managed to accommodate 1,611 and the other 100 patients were sent to the Hospital Annex at Otsu, Japan, which had opened on 8 October 1950 as a convalescent unit for Naval Hospital Yokosuka and had a 400-bed capacity.

November had a slow but steady flow of patients, including 796 admissions and 268 evacuations. By 30 November, 1,402 patients were on the sick list, of which 544 were battle casualties.[24]

Buildings were still being converted into hospital spaces when Chief Nurse Burke wrote:

A receiving barracks of Commander Fleet Activities was converted into wards. Navy personnel were transferred from their barracks to nearby Camp McGill, an army post.

We had been informed that we were receiving 250 ambulatory patients. Before night[fall] 850 exhausted, cold, and hungry marines had been admitted to Barracks B. This building is located one quarter of a mile from the main hospital. All medications, equipment, supplies and linen had to be supplied via trucks.

Many of these patients had only one sheet over the mattress cover and a blanket. Five navy nurses, three medical officers and eleven hospital corpsmen took care of them . . . that day.

Practically every patient was suffering from frostbite, either solely or in combination with gunshot wounds. Each received penicillin as part of his treatment. One nurse gave these penicillin injections almost continuously throughout the day.

And more nurses were on their way . . .

Photo courtesy of Virginia Jennings Watson

The Point is a key landmark for ships entering Yokosuka Harbor.

A woman is like a teabag.
You never know how strong it is until it's in hot water.

Eleanor Roosevelt

3

Patients Arriving

Chosin Reservoir

The morning of 27 November 1950 was bright and clear and very, very cold. We looked to our front to see what caused the disturbance last evening. There was a dead Chinese officer [with] a tape measure. I remember wondering if they were surveying our position.

The patrol was about squad size. We went down to the reservoir, walked parallel to it for a short distance . . . then went northwest and back to the company. No contact was made. But we did see numerous footprints [indicating] twenty to thirty men were in the area to the north of our position.

Photo courtesy of First Marine Division
Chosin Reservoir – U.S. Marines attack during breakout from Hagaru-ri.

About 2300 (11:00 PM) the attack started again. We fired the remainder of our ammo. There was a short lull. Then the attack was returned with greater intensity than before.

The Chinese probing had apparently found the point between Bey's and Yancey's platoons. [This is where] they concentrated their attack . . . . There were mortars and grenades falling on our position. I saw six to eight Chinese coming toward [us]. I fired at them and stopped them momentarily. Then about a half dozen grenades exploded around my hole.

I ducked down until they stopped exploding. When I looked up there were about twenty Chinese coming toward me. I fired some more but couldn't stop them.

There were many grenades thrown, perhaps mortars also. It seemed to me that the Chinese were dragging baskets full of grenades along behind them. They would reach in and throw one, then reach in and throw another and another and another.

The Chinese apparently had illuminating grenades. They would work their way very close to our lines.. throw several illuminating grenades and survey the area . . . then throw offensive concussion grenades and move forward.

The effect was eerie, with a yellow-white light reflecting off the snow [and the] Chinese looked ghost-like in their white parka uniforms.

The explosions were all around me. I felt a sting in my left leg but otherwise I was lucky. We stopped them briefly but they regrouped and came on again. This time I wasn't so lucky. I was hit hard in the arm, wrist and chest by [shrapnel from] two or three grenades.

I crawled back to the CP [command post] to get a bandage on my wrist [which] was bleeding profusely. The corpsman bandaged my wrist. I started back up the hill but discovered I had a great deal of difficulty walking. I didn't think my wrist would cause all that difficulty. What I did not know at the time was that I had two pieces of shrapnel in my chest, my lung had collapsed and my chest was filled with fluid. Try as I might, I just couldn't function.

So I sat down again [and] asked the corpsman if he could do anything. He said there was an aid station just down the trail. They could get me there.

I staggered and stumbled to the aid station. Instead of first aid, they put me on a stretcher, bandaged me up [and] gave me a shot of morphine. That was the end of my activity at the Chosin Reservoir.

On 28 November 1950, I went by helicopter to Hagaru-ri [and] spent

two days [at a field hospital] during heavy attacks. It seemed as if the
Chinese attacked all night. Bullets were hitting the building, splattering
plaster all around the room. Recoilless rifles were shooting constantly,
rattling everything with a deafening roar.

On 1 December, I was flown to Naval Hospital Yokosuka, Japan.[25]

1st Lt. William J. Schreier, USMC

Photo courtesy of Navy Bureau of Medicine and Surgery Archives (BUMED)
The Fifth and Seventh Marines reorganize at Yudam-ni after fighting off the Chinese divisions.
they began a five-day battle over fifteen icy miles back to Hagaru-ri.
Temperatures fell to twenty-five degrees below zero. 29 November 1950.

During the end of November and early December the battle in the Chosin
Reservoir raged on. Consequently, Naval Hospital Yokosuka experienced the
heaviest patient load in December 1950, an average of 191.1 new patients per
day with admissions totaling 5,927.

Sgt. John Joseph Vincent Cook, USMC (Ret), known as J.J.V.C. and Cookie,
was assigned to Machine Gun Platoon, C Company, First Marine Division. He
was hospitalized with hepatitis at Naval Hospital Yokosuka:

In late November the wards and hallways were full of beds and pa-
tients. The atmosphere at the hospital turned from bright to gloom when
[so many wounded and so many] types of wounds were exposed to all
hands.

The navy nurses and corpsmen showed their courage in the way they handled this deluge of serious cases. Always bright, cheerful, professional and with kind words. This is something that cannot be described. It's something that one does not forget after fifty years.

The doctor, nurse and corpsman that I was in close contact with were Lt.(jg) A. V. Holmes, Ens. Anne Hopple, and Hospital Corpsman Portis Hatcher. I had the most contact with these three people. I remember them the most. I must say that all the hospital hands were the GREATEST! Even the Japanese janitor, "Ouija."

I was discharged to Otsu replacement center 7 January 1951. I returned to C Company, was assigned to Second Rifle Platoon on 26 January 1951 and completed my tour in Korea in August 1951.

Photo courtesy of Navy Bureau of Medicine and Surgery Archives (BUMED)
For five days and nights in subzero weather, from 28 November to 3 December, U.S. Marines fought back fifteen miles through Chinese troops to Hagaru-ri on the southern tip of Chosin Reservoir.

On 4 December 1950, wounded 2d Lt. Joseph R. Owen began to make his trek from Chosin Reservoir to Yokosuka Naval Hospital:

The morphine had worn off. . . . People were carrying me from the ditch on a stretcher. The pain came in great, twisting stabs. [My buddy] Kelly was there. His iced-coated, filthy face was close to mine. Two of them lifted me into the ambulance. They grunted as they put me into a top rack. "This one is a big fucker."

The ambulance had dark canvas bulkheads stained with clots of blood . . . now frozen and crusted with frost. The racks were filled with wounded men. The one below me screamed for morphine. Another moaned and cursed, softly. I shivered with cold. A corpsman threw a blanket over me.

The ride back to the aid station was over a rutted, frozen mud road. We jostled and bounced. I was afraid that I would be jarred from my rack. With every lurch came a searing jolt of pain.

There was a whiff of shit. I must have let go in my pants. Then there was a jab somewhere on my body. I soon felt warmth and the pain softened.

A blast of cold air hit my face and I was awake again. I hurt terribly. I was not in heaven, not even dead. I was again on a stretcher. Two men were carrying me up a ramp into a cargo plane.

There were long rows of racks inside the hold of the plane. The racks were filled with stretcher cases. The walking wounded sat on the benches in the middle. Their bandage wrapped heads and arms were stained with blood.

The next time I woke I thought I was in hell! It was a huge, open ward filled with cots. Wounded men in the cots were covered with brown army blankets. The place was noisy with calls of, "Medic!" The army call their corpsmen "medic."

The pain was there. My right arm was wrapped up big as a watermelon, tubes going into the ends. On the other shoulder and across my chest there were thick bandages and wide strips of tape. The only thing I could move was my left arm below the elbow. I could barely wiggle the fingers of that hand. I couldn't get it out from under the blanket. I called out, "Corpsman!" I wanted a real doc, not a medic.

About 8 December 1950 Owen finally arrived at Naval Hospital Yokosuka:

I was awake after an ambulance ride into the Yokosuka Naval Hospital. Two Japanese orderlies rolled me on a gurney through long corridors. They turned into an officers' ward.

Photo courtesy of Navy Bureau of Medicine and Surgery Archives (BUMED)
The cold harsh weather in the Chosin Reservoir caused severe frostbite.

During the forty-eight-hour period of 6 and 7 December, a total of 2,022 patients were admitted. Just about this time, Gy. Sgt. William H. Yarnall, I Company, Third Battalion, First Marines, arrived at Naval Hospital Yokosuka. He was evacuated sometime between 27 November 1950 and 1 December 1950. His first stop was an army hospital in Japan:

> *At Yokosuka Naval Hospital, I was put in a hallway. I was told that there were no beds at the moment. Between the nurses and the corpsmen, it didn't matter about the hallway. They made it seem like the Ritz Hotel. If we made one moan . . . a nurse and a corpsman were immediately at our side.*
>
> *The overall treatment I received from the hands of our navy nurses was the best. There are no words to make my feelings known to you, save to say, God bless the naval nursing corps. You all deserve the Medal of Honor.*

Operating Room

Lt. Helen Fable, a surgical nurse, arrived at Naval Hospital Yokosuka on 23 December 1950:

> *My first day of duty, I was assigned to Ward O. After what seemed like hours of walking the halls, a corpsman stopped and gave me directions.*

Ward O was located on a balcony above the obstetrical ward. The patients were mostly ambulatory and waiting for transfer to a rehab unit in Osaka. When the chief nurse discovered I was an OR [operating room] nurse, I was immediately transferred to the OR.

The staff in the OR varied between five and eight nurses. There were usually eight to ten corpsmen. When the Fleet Marines brought in casualties, their corpsmen came along. We used them in the OR, so the number of corpsmen could vary between seventeen and twenty.

I was very impressed with the professional training that the corpsmen had received in surgical procedures. The corpsmen with the Fleet Marines were very well trained and very good.

Because of the number of casualties, at that time, duty days in the OR lasted seventy-two to ninety-six hours without a break. After about three months, it settled down. We went back to an eight-hour duty.

For the first two or three months we had trains coming in with patients every two to three hours. We had triage in the halls, there were patients on stretchers lined up, waiting to come in and we had only three operating tables.

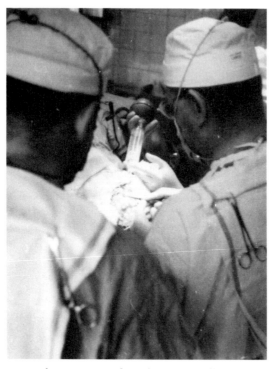

Photo courtesy of Marilyn Ewing Affleck

Doctors prepare for brain surgery.

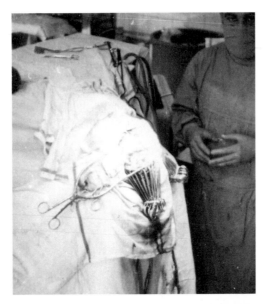

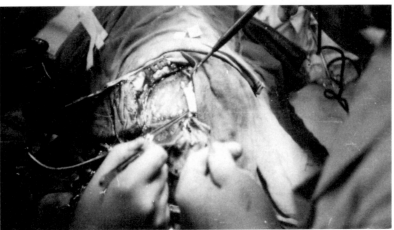

Photos courtesy of Marilyn Ewing Affleck

Due to numerous incidents of head wounds, brain surgery was a frequent procedure.

Fable and the surgical team worked at a furious pace:

> We'd have them lined up for hours [and] we got them out as fast as we could. We'd have three tables going on the same time. It was like M*A*S*H (the television show) [but] I think we had better conditions and we didn't have Klinger. I was very proud of my nurses and corpsmen. I'd do it all over again if I got the chance.

Due to the subzero temperatures, ranging from minus thirty to forty, frostbite became a constant battle. It was prevalent throughout the war zone and affected the extremities like the hands and feet. According to the U.S. Armed Forces Medical Journal:[26]

> *Most of the cases occurred as the result of a tactical situation . . . the soldier was immobilized from two to twenty-four hours by enemy action . . . the ambient temperature ranging from twenty degrees to minus thirty degrees Fahrenheit.*
>
> *Wet feet, inadequate protection and exhaustion . . . severe climatic conditions . . . immobility for several hours appears to be the most important factors in the production of ground-type frostbite.*

The USAFMJ says:

> *First degree frostbite is characterized by numbness, swelling and erythema [redness] of the involved part.*
>
> *Second degree frostbite produces vesiculation [blistering or peeling] of the skin. This involves only partial skin thickness.*
>
> *Third degree frostbite involves the entire thickness of skin and [sometimes goes deeper into the] tissues. The most common sites for this degree of injury [are] at the great toes, second toes, heels, and tips of the fingers.*
>
> *Fourth degree frostbite . . . extends through the entire thickness of the [skin and includes the] bone. Fourth degree frostbite results in [amputation] . . . of an extremity or part of it.[27]*

Nurses and corpsmen treated frostbite routinely. They washed the affected area thoroughly with soap and lukewarm water, painted it with merthiolate, excised blistered and dead tissues and clipped or removed nails if the blister extended under the nail bed. They applied oxide ointment to lesions and dispensed penicillin to prevent infections. To ease pain, sometimes they applied a mild anesthetic ointment directly to the affected area. They gave patients aspirin to reduce aching pain. Then they wrapped each toe with plain gauze dressing. Patients walked to meals and to the head (bathroom) to stimulate circulation.[28]

Due to the constant fighting in the field, patients were not brought immediately to medical facilities. When they arrived, the blisters were old, dried out, hard, purple and infected. Lack of circulation in the blackened, rotted flesh could lead to gangrene. Amputation was the last resort.

Patients wounded in the field were transported in helicopters with open-air baskets and, in many cases, exposure during these flights caused frostbite.

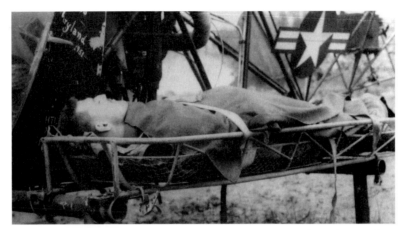

Photo courtesy of Navy Bureau of Medicine and Surgery Archives (BUMED)
Flying in open baskets on helicopters put the injured at risk for frostbite.

Although the soldiers worried about their wounds, frostbite threatened them more.

Marines were instructed to guard against frostbite, but in subzero weather it was often unavoidable. Many times the marines focused on other injuries, not realizing they had frostbite. Marine Second Lieutenant Owen tried to have his men use preventative measures:

> Frostbite came quickly in the wind-driven, sub-zero cold of the North Korean mountains. The shoe-pacs we wore were clunky canvas and leather that trapped the . . . sweat in our heavy woolen socks when we were on the move. When we stopped, the cold got into the shoe-pacs and the sweat froze. We tried to keep our toes moving for circulation, especially when we were pinned down by enemy fire or were otherwise immobile.
>
> Every night, regardless of the temperature, I ordered my men to take off their shoe-pacs and put on . . . dry socks. We had not been trained for cold-weather fighting. Those tricks we learned later, after we lost as many men to frostbite as to gunshot wounds. Frostbite could mean amputated toes.

Because of the massive influx of patients, standard hospital beds were replaced with double-and triple-deck beds. Personnel from the Receiving Station worked day and night to complete this task.

Gy. Sgt. Carroll V. Schmidt, USMCR, who served with the First Battalion Seventh Marines, was recalled to active duty just after the marines came out of the trap at Chosin Reservoir, and was severely wounded:

I would have died right there on patrol if it had not been for the good corpsman with us. We always called him Doc. They told me at the aid station that if Doc and Mason [my marine buddy who found me] had not applied the pressure bandages on my wound, I would not have made it . . . Doc and Mason saved my life.

On a routine day the doctor and the nurses would check to see how we were doing. If for any reason during the day or night we needed help, there was always someone right there.

One of the things that made our ward seem better was the refrigerator. It was always stocked with fruit, milk, etc. We were welcome to it any time. If we were unable to get to it, the nurse or corpsman would bring [the food] to our beds.

Like the fellow in the bed next to me said, "Bet our congressmen stateside don't have it this good."

The doctor and nurses that were with us most of the time never got much rest. You hear people say, "Our door is always open to you!" On our ward it was a fact. If the doctor and nurses were not treating patients, they were there. Any time anyone wanted to talk to them, they could. They always had time to answer questions. I know that many days they worked around fourteen to fifteen hours.

Orthopedic Ward

Comdr. Betty Jo Alexander, Nurse Corps, U.S. Navy (Ret), known to her friends as Alex, worked in the orthopedic ward as an ensign:

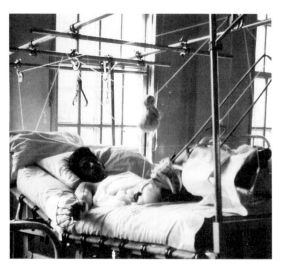

Photo courtesy of Jean Ellis Young
Balanced traction units, as shown, were used to properly align broken bones.
After the bone was set in place, a cast was put on. This patient has a fractured femur.

I remember that the Orthopedic Department had double and triple bunk beds. The critically injured patients were on the lower bunks, and the more ambulatory patients were on the upper bunks.

We saw a lot of multiple fractures and a lot of injuries due to land mines. They would get into a landmine and then step backwards or sideways into another one. There were a lot of limbs lost.

For a period of time Alexander and Ewing worked as ensigns in the orthopedic ward. Later Alexander worked in the psychiatric ward where she was in charge of insulin and shock therapy. While assigned to the orthopedic ward, Ewing found it challenging and rewarding:

The hardest part was the amputees. I'll never forget this one young marine who was in such anguish. Not because of his own physical pain of losing both forearms, but he recalled how his older brother had gone off in World War II and lost both his arms. He didn't tell his family and when he returned home his family had been utterly shocked.

So my patient's pain was not for himself, but for his family. He did not want to hurt them again by telling them what happened to him during the Korean War.

M. Sgt. Thaddeus A. Laird, USMC (Ret), recalled arriving in the spring of 1951 at Naval Hospital Yokosuka:

On or about 4 April 1951, I left the First Battalion, Fifth Marines, First Marine Division. I was on rotation from Korea. In the interim I felt really sick. I was sent to a field hospital with infectious hepatitis and jaundice. I was sent to the Haven [and] then to a ward at Yokosuka Naval Hospital.

I have great memories of a nurse that we called "Miss Frances." She cut about two pounds of skin callous off my feet. As she did this she said, "I guess you're in the infantry." She was dark haired and very caring and a good nurse. I thought highly of my "Miss Frances."

The back rubs became very popular, of course, as the patients began to feel better:

While at Yokosuka Hospital, each evening about 1800 (6:00 PM) Miss Chumley would come into our ward . . . with a bottle of liniment to give the patients back rubs. She was a gorgeous blond nurse from Kentucky.

It was comical to see the patients jump in their bunks. "Me next, Miss Chumley." I was lucky and got a back rub.

1st Sgt. Andrew Peter Boquet, USMC (Ret)

Photo courtesy of Lois Merritt

Three nurses well represented their respective services in the Far East March of Dimes campaign. Lt.(jg) Nell Chumley (front), stationed at Yokosuka Naval Hospital, reigns as Navy Polio Queen; 1st Lt. Ave Dittman (left) represents USAF; and 1st Lt. Anne Jablunovsky (right) represents the army. (U.S. Navy photo)

Lt. Comdr. Jean Ellis Young, Navy Nurse Corps, U.S. Navy (Ret), remembers that patient care was a very important part of the care provided at Naval Hospital Yokosuka:

> *There was an incident where a patient had a hip spica, a body cast that sometimes also encases the legs. A metal rod is placed between the legs to keep them apart in the cast.*
>
> *This patient was experiencing irritation under the cast, causing abrasions under the cast and bleeding. To remedy this, I had to cut a window in the cast to alleviate further abrasions.*

Pfc Raul Rendon, USMC (Ret), describes life in a spica cast:

> *I was wounded on 27 November 1950 at the Chosin Reservoir . . . hit while firing the gun in thirty degrees below zero. Four of my buddies at Yudam-ni . . . carried [me] in a poncho. The navy doctor . . . at a makeshift night aid station . . . gave me blood and cut the frozen bandages. He put chemical pads on my belly and covered me up with blankets*

The doctors and corpsmen had a hell of a time trying to work at thirty degrees below zero. They forgot about the chemical pad on my belly so it burned me and I have a large scar. Still on a stretcher, I was put in a helicopter . . . not equipped to carry wounded like they showed [on] the television show M*A*S*H. So my body was half in and half was out of the chopper. I was tied down . . . on morphine so I did not feel the burning pain . . . or just didn't give a damn. [We] flew about eighty miles south to Hamhong, North Korea, First Army MASH. It was already the wee hours of 28 November 1950.

Days later I flew to Japan and Naval Hospital Yokosuka. My doctor . . . a reserve commander . . . and medical professor . . . named Robert was called in because he was a urologist. I named one of my sons "Robert."

One morning I was taking inventory of myself. I was in a hell of a mess . . . wounded in both hips through and through . . . a burn on my belly . . . frostbite on both feet, nose, ears, and fingers on both hands. But my feet were the worst..

I was in a full body cast, both legs apart. I was given a coat hanger to scratch under my cast. I could not even clean my tail. I had tubes in me and both feet were black with frostbite and gangrene. Then I had an allergic reaction to penicillin.

In Yokosuka Hospital, the nurses and corpsmen called me Fred Astaire. Even though I was in a body cast, my right foot . . . kept moving . . . even when I was sleeping.

Because of my frostbite, I got three shots of brandy, one at each meal. But I didn't care for it, so the corpsmen asked if they could have it. I wanted candy instead. So they got me a box of Bit-o-Honey and a box of Mars bars.

The nurses always came over to see if there was anything we needed. They tried to comfort us, especially the marines like me who could not move.

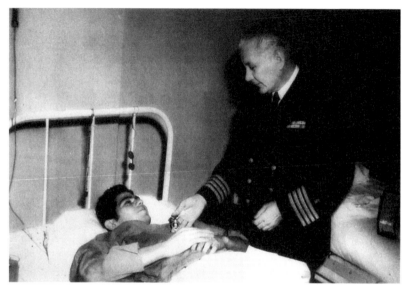

Photo courtesy of Raul Rendon
Pfc Raul Rendon, USMC, receives the Purple Heart from Capt. W.F. James, MC, USN.

U. S. NAVAL HOSPITAL
NAVY NO. 3923
c/o F. P. O. SAN FRANCISCO, CALIF.

NH3923/P6-1/2

JAN 3   1951

From: Commanding Officer
To :   RENDON, Raul R., Pfc, 633061, USMC

Subj :   Purple Heart; awarding of

Ref :   (a) AlNav 96-50

Encl :   (1) Purple Heart Medal

1.   In the name of the President of the United States and as authorized by reference (a),
you are hereby awarded the Purple Heart Medal for wounds received in action against the
enemy on _____27 November 1950_____ in the Korean Theatre of operations.

W. F. JAMES

Copy to:
ComNavFE
Bu Pers

Rendon's Purple Heart citation.

4

And Kept On Coming

Naval Hospital Yokosuka provided an appropriate location, potential expansion capabilities, and existing infrastructure for treating casualties from the Far East Command. The Japanese naval base was selected for CFAY because of its comprehensive facilities, and the U.S. would discover that there were exceptional security measures in place: a network of caves and tunnels.

The Caves, Pre War

Prior to World War II, as tensions grew internationally, the Japanese were concerned about protecting their assets.[29] They valued their shipbuilding and repair capability and most of it was located at the then Japanese-owned base and shipyard at Yokosuka. Early in 1940 the Japanese constructed on the base a huge command center, in a cave known as C-39, that included an underground tunnel system that connected to the main headquarters buildings C-1 and C-2.

As World War II dragged on and the bombing raids increased, the Japanese feared heavy air strikes. They feared the shipyard and base would be hit in retaliation for their bombing of Pearl Harbor, so in 1943 they focused on constructing air raid shelters.

Because no power machinery was available, they dug caves into the hillside manually using volunteers and civilian shipyard employees who wanted overtime work. In a few months the hillside on the main base was full of tunnels leading to entrances to underground rooms that ranged in size from six by twelve feet to thirty by forty feet.

By mid-1944 there was believed to be about sixteen miles of underground networks that were used as air raid shelters. As the war intensified, many offices dealing with military operations were moved into the caves and so the caves became offices, workspaces, and factories:

The main personnel department cave [was] adjacent to the underground
command center . . . a multi-branch cavern leading to several rooms. It
was large enough to accommodate 800 workers.[30]

The Caves, During the War

There were what some called "close moments" while they were stationed at
Naval Hospital Yokosuka, but the fighting continued to be away from
Yokosuka. As far as those interviewed remembered, the facilities at Yokosuka
were never attacked.

Most were aware that they were living on the fringe of the war zone, but they
did not have time to be frightened. There was just so much to do. Patients were arriving at a swift and unrelenting pace and they were uppermost in nurses' minds.

In the event that CFAY was attacked, the navy's contingency plan was that
the nurses and corpsmen would move the patients into the caves. There was one
cave located on a hill adjacent to the hospital:

> *I can remember going to the cave only once, during a false alarm.*
> *Patients who couldn't be moved we had to leave on the ward. Nurses and*
> *corpsmen stayed with the orthopedic patients . . . the patients in traction.*
> *The caves were well set up. There were no beds so we had to take the pa-*
> *tients on stretchers, which were placed across rails that lined the walls.*
>
> **Lt. Comdr. Fable, USN (Ret)**

> *I remember those caves. But I never made it to them. We were on alert.*
> *And when the air raid attack warning sounded, we'd start to head for*
> *the cave. Every time we got out the door, it was all over, so I never saw*
> *inside them.*
>
> **Comdr. Merritt, USN (Ret)**

To this day Sgt. George Maling, USMC, has retained his hospital tag from
when he was a patient in Ward K at Yokosuka Naval Hospital. The tag shows his
name, rank, serial number and date of admission (5 January 1953); his doctors
as Linski and Phelan; and, in case of an evacuation, he was assigned to Cave 18,
Section A-Red-E.

Anyone who has ever been aboard a navy ship knows that drills are not always conducted during the workday. To simulate reality, they come at all
hours. Usually it's in the middle of the night or early morning. Ewing recalled it
was no different at Yokosuka:

The air raid siren went off in the middle of the night. This was after we had all gone to bed. It had been an exhausting day. We must have been sound asleep. We were just so tired. So when the siren sounded we all jumped up. When you are so stunned, it takes a minute. Then you figure out what to do. Sometimes you don't exactly know what you are doing. Then we remembered: run for the cave.

There was all this excitement and confusion. One of the nurses did not know what to do. Should she quickly put on her false eyelashes or something else. Anyway, we beat feet to the cave. I don't remember the patients being with us.

Photo courtesy of Lee Jacobson
Photo taken in 1945 shows the openings to the caves built by the Japanese
(background, to the left of Navy Supply Depot). Hammerhead crane built in 1934 lifted equipment
off the three hospital ships during the Korean War.

The Wards

The hospital wards at Yokosuka were designated alphabetically. Ward V, or Victor, was the orthopedic ward where Ewing worked. Other wards included neurosurgery, psychiatric, family practice, SOQ (Sick Officers' Quarters).

HMSC John McCloskey, USN (Ret), enlisted in the navy on 5 February 1946:

I went to the recruiting station in downtown Pittsburgh. I believe I signed the papers for two years. I recall that the recruiter asked me about my skills. I couldn't think of any. He said, "I have yeoman and corpsman open." "What are they?" I asked. "You are now a corpsman," he answered.

McCloskey served from 1946 until 1948. In June 1950, as a navy reservist, he was recalled to active duty and received orders to Naval Hospital Yokosuka. McCloskey was assigned to Ward C:

Primarily Ward C was a neurological service. At different times we had a variety of patients. This was true especially during the Chosin Reservoir period.

We trained at Hospital Corpsman "A" School. What we did during the Korean War was all OJT (on-the-job-training).

Normal ward duties, considering the times, were TPRs, changing dressing . . . giving medications . . . shots . . . bed baths . . . enemas, etc. Some of the ward cleaning was done by the ambulatory patients.

One of the unusual things I had to do was dispense shots of liquor to frostbite patients. The nurses held the narcotic locker keys. This is where the liquor bottles were kept. Walking through the ward with one ounce shot glasses on a tray could be an adventure. Some frost bite patients wanted the booze. Some wouldn't touch the stuff. There were plenty of marines without frostbite looking for the leftovers.

During the Chosin period we had a number of bunks on the ward. The patients on the top bunks were ambulatory. But I tried to accommodate them: I climbed up so they wouldn't have to climb down. Since they had to have shots in the morning and evening, I thought I'd save them a trip.

Except for accompanying paraplegic evacuations, we all pitched in. Ward duties were performed by the corpsmen and the nurses as needed.

Things were busy one day. I remember one nurse defrosting/cleaning the Treatment Room refrigerator. The nurses supervised the Ward Record Room and the Treatment Room. The only nurse I can recall is Ms. Danko.

The camaraderie among the Ward C staff was, probably, the best that I have ever experienced. Everyone worked together.

The corpsmen worked port and starboard . . . 0700 to 2100 one day . . . the next day, from 0700 to 1500. I worked night duty from 2100 until 0700 for one or two months. We worked one weekend. We were off the next weekend. We had "Cinderella" liberty. We had to be back aboard the base at midnight.

Photo courtesy of John McCloskey
Corpsmen at Naval Hospital Yokosuka posed outside Ward C. Bottom step,
left HM3 John McCloskey with Harlan, Maxwell, Feaschette.

Col. John J. Peeler, USMC (Ret), recounts suffering multiple shrapnel wounds on the nights of 26 and 27 March 1953. He spent a short time onboard one of the hospital ships and was then flown to Yokosuka where he remained for about six weeks:

The nurse I remember particularly [was] Lt. Tommy Thompson. She was a full lieutenant . . . an attractive redhead in her mid-twenties. All the nurses were tremendous . . . but she always seemed to want to go the extra mile to take care of her patients . . . with a ready smile no matter how tired she must have been. She had a great sense of humor.

Tommy saw to it that I was able to radio-phone my wife. This was shortly after I got to the hospital. As I was a bed patient, she got the phone to my bed.

The nurses could not do enough for us. We knew they truly cared about us. They gave us the best treatment possible, and I saw them cry when a patient died.

Photo courtesy of Carola Braun Gradilone
Ward E nurses. (Left to right) Helen Sekin, Carola Braun, Peg Heimberger, Jane Small.

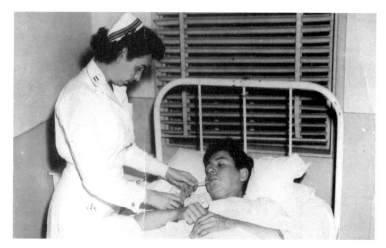

Photo courtesy of Gilbert Towner
Pfc Gilbert Towner remembers being the 10,000 patient at Naval Hospital Yokosuka.

Hospital Corpsmen

Of all the personnel in navy medicine, the nurses probably knew the navy hospital corpsmen the best. They supervised and trained the corpsmen. The nurses also worked closely with them in a crisis. Comdr. Florence Alwyn (Twyman) remembers the corpsmen with whom she worked:

> *I can't say enough about the caliber of corpsmen. For the most part they had experience. They were not fresh out of corpsman school. I was a charge nurse. This was on a surgical ward. The corpsmen worked exceptionally hard. They knew what was expected of them.*

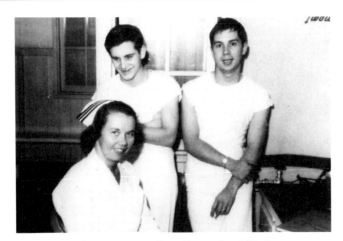

Photo courtesy of Marilyn Ewing Affleck
(Left to right) Ewing and Hospital Corpsmen George Cardinal and Les Grahak
are on night duty in Ward V.

The Bureau of Navy Medicine and Surgery provided hospital corpsmen for the U.S. Marines in the field. There always has been a special bond between the corpsmen and the marines, who lovingly refer to their corpsmen as "Doc":

> *All marines would look out for Doc, the corpsman. No one would mess with a corpsman at all. He is the one that we call out [for] when we get hit. He comes flying to us. When on liberty, if we see a corpsman in a bar drinking, he does not have to pay for another drink. The marines take care of the bill. We keep an eye out, so no one messes with the Doc.*
>
> **Pfc Paul Rendon, USMC (Ret)**

Rendon remembers his corpsman in the field:

> *Bill Davis was the corpsman who patched me up under fire. He asked where it hurt. I said, "My right hip." He cut off the clothing, patched me up, and gave me morphine. It was thirty degrees below zero, so he had to keep the morphine ampoules in his mouth. Soon more marines were getting hit. Bill was working about eight to ten feet from where I was lying when he got hit in the face by a mortar.*
>
> *In 1985, I saw him at a reunion of the Chosin Few in San Diego.*

Then there was his corpsman at Naval Hospital Yokosuka:

> *One corpsman used to make us laugh. He'd act like a monkey. Walk like one . . . arms hanging low . . . making monkey noises . . . and act like he*

was removing lice from his body and eating them. I still laugh when I think about it.

Petty Officer Adams was Rendon's "monkey" corpsman. Rendon has kept a picture and fond memories of his corpsmen for almost fifty years.

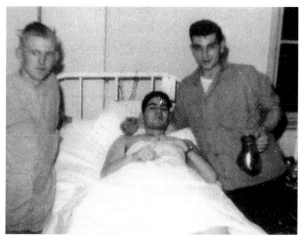

Photo courtesy of Raul Rendon
(Left to right) Corpsmen Adams, Rendon, and Corpsman Frank.

The corpsmen always tried to go the extra mile to make life a little easier for those under their care:

A rundown building was used as the division hospital in Korea and it was filled with a sad bunch of marines. They had dysentery, frostbite and other problems. Those great corpsmen opened large tins of alcohol and cans of grapefruit juice and filled all the canteen cups. I will never forget it. I'm sure that kept the troops spirits from going into the dumps.
Sgt. Donald Phillips, USMC (Ret)

Recovering

As Rendon and others found out, the nurses on the wards were vigilant and keenly aware of what the patients did all the time:

All the nurses went out of their way to help us. I began to recover slowly, but I was still in the body cast. The patients were passing some dirty stories and I was reading some typed sheets of paper when the nurse came to me. "What are you reading?" I folded the sheets of paper and answered, "A letter from home." I did not fool her. She looked at me and told me to be careful.

And of course the patients did not miss anything either, Rendon wrote:

This nurse, a lieutenant, was a good nurse. When she was talking to someone she had the habit of pulling on the rubber elastic of her panty. She always pulled the elastic on her right thigh and let it go, so we could hear a snap. We all kept an eye on that!

Pfc Herbert Luster recalls how, as the marines got better, they would try to get the nurses' attention:

We used to lie in bed and try to think of ways to get the nurses' attention. A line a lot of marines used was, "Nurse, nurse, I'm worse. Call a hearse."

Major Maiden will never live down one of his experiences at Naval Hospital Yokosuka:

I will never forget one day at Yokosuka. We were getting ready to go on liberty when they announced the new doctor was doing an inspection and wanted to visit with all patients. We were dressed to head out on liberty, so several of us jumped into our beds with our uniforms on and awaited the new doctor.

When he got to our room. I had the covers pulled up as far as I could. I described my wounds to him. He grasped the covers and pulled them down. There was a young lieutenant all dressed to go on liberty.

As nurses, corpsmen and patients discovered, sometimes laughter and silliness are good remedies for stressful situations:

Life didn't always impart an air of dignity in Ward K. The evening I arrived at the ward in the Naval Hospital in Yokosuka, there was a nurse laughing a little hysterically in a wheel chair; she was being pushed around the ward by two crazy-acting marines.

Sgt. Donald Phillips, USMC (Ret)

A Hand on Humanity

War's frenzy brings out the worst in humans. Men are forced, ordered to kill those they don't know. It's part of war. But sometimes unusual things happen that rise from the soul and go beyond the moment and penetrate deep into our humanity:

One afternoon Ewing was talking to one of her patients:

He said all the guys he was with had been killed, so he lay on the field, hoping the North Koreans would think he was dead. After awhile, they left.

But the North Koreans came back and found him alive. The marine was convinced that they would kill him, but instead they picked him up, carried him to the middle of the field, then went back into the brush. No one fired on him. He lay there. He heard the Whup! Whup! Whup! of a helicopter. The North Koreans let the helicopter land, the marine was picked up, and taken to safety. It was almost as if time had stood still for a moment. For one rational moment. And the humanity embedded in the souls of these men prevailed.

Others had similar experiences:

While I was at Yokosuka a great big sailor was in my ward who had encephalitis. He was unconscious and being worked on by a couple of doctors. The docs said he was dead.

Mrs. Green, a naval nurse, was watching. She refused to give up. She continued to revive the sailor. She did. She brought him back from the dead. Needless to say she was regarded as a hero in our ward. As I recall she was about thirty-five years of age. She had dark hair and an ordinary build. I hope she got an award for her actions.

1st Sgt. Andrew Peter Boquet, USMC (Ret)

Waiting to say thanks

Until now, many of the marines have not been able to tell their stories. Their physical pain was easier to forget than their inability to say thank you. So for fifty years they have been haunted and lived with the pain that they never expressed their gratitude. They didn't know their nurses names. That was the frustrating part. Now the marines are telling their stories for their nurses, to say thank you.

I was at Yokosuka. I wish I remembered names of the nurses. I will always carry a fondness for them. They helped me during a dismal period of my life. It was pounded into marines to always show respect of rank. However, the nurses broke down that barrier . . . with their sympathetic, warmhearted approach.

Sgt. Donald Phillips, USMC (Ret)

Their genuine dedication and professionalism and caring for the wounded stands out in my mind. You ladies provided more than our rehabilitation. You provided a personal touch of human kindness and concern. That accounts for my memories of those days long ago in Yokosuka.

We were like family . . . if only for a short time. I shall not forget the days you made better by caring for those of us in your care. Thanks a million and thanks for the memories. Semper Fi.

Maj. Robert Maiden USMC, (Ret)

As I look back, I say job well done. You are our heroes!

Cpl. Robert Goode, USMC (Ret)

Photo courtesy of Marilyn Ewing Affleck
Robert Calhoun, USMC, (arm in cast) attends a USO show at Naval Hospital Yokosuka.

To have a good friend is one of the highest delights of life;
to be a good friend is one of the noblest
and most difficult undertakings.

Anonymous

⟫ 5 ⟪

Home Sweet Yokosuka

Team Yokosuka

Light is the task when many share the toil.

Homer, Iliad

When the Korean War broke out in June 1950, it was obvious that Naval Hospital Yokosuka had to expand. Medical personnel from various navy commands were pulled in from both the east and west coasts and sent immediately to Naval Hospital Yokosuka. Medical personnel represented a diversity of backgrounds, yet they all came together, as one. It was Team Yokosuka that overcame insurmountable odds to accomplish mission during the Korean War. By 1951, over 10,000 patients had been treated in what had been a one hundred-bed hospital less than a year earlier.[31]

Photo courtesy of Marilyn Ewing Affleck
Medical staff of Ward V. (Left to right) Dr. Francis, Lt.(jg) Marilyn Ewing, Dr. William Strong,
Lt. Dorothy Lukowski, Lt. Ruth Scanlon, HN William Price, Lt.(jg) Jean Ellis,
and Hospital Corpsman Besemar (kneeling).

The medical team at Naval Hospital Yokosuka was just that, a team.

It did not matter whose job it was. If a bedpan needed to be changed, it was done. Each bedpan had to be rinsed. Sometimes it was scrubbed and put in a steam hopper. It was done. It didn't matter who did it.

When the patients got better, they helped. They assisted the corpsmen and [the nurses]. They helped care for their buddies. The marines just pitched in. If they saw something needed to be done . . . they'd do it. You never had to ask those boys. They were great!

Lt. Virginia Jennings, NC, USN

Chief Nurse Burke took great pride in her Team Yokosuka.

During a two-week period the night supervisor assisted in patient admission . . . to expedite . . . admission of the critically ill patients [and to] expedite [their] care. Many nights litter patients were lined up along the full length of the corridor.

On one of the medical wards, nurses assisted [with] serving trays to approximately 225 patients at each meal. During the second and third week after admission, many patients had second and third servings of food at each meal. This was the equivalent of 675 patients.

Photo courtesy of Navy Bureau of Medicine and Surgery Archives (BUMED)
Lt. Comdr. Alberta Burk, chief nurse, was responsible for the rapid conversion of a 100-bed dispensary in Yokosuka into a hospital caring for over 5,000 patients. Shown here with Gerda Agerholm (rank equivalent to major) at a reception for the Danish hospital ship *Jutlandia*.

With the influx of patients, the Japanese nationals definitely became part of Team Yokosuka. They worked at the shipyard, on the base, as well as in the hospital complex. Young Japanese maids were assigned to the nurses' quarters to do the nurses' personal laundry, clean the quarters, and sometimes cook. The maids were affectionately called "girl-sans."

Photo courtesy of Marilyn Ewing Affleck
Lieutenant Alexander poses outside the nurses' quarters with two of the "girl-sans" who cleaned the nurses' rooms and washed their clothes.

Stryker frames

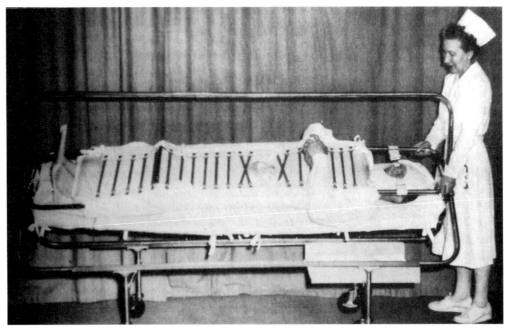

Photo courtesy of Navy Bureau of Medicine and Surgery Archives (BUMED)
Stryker frames are used to turn paraplegic and quadriplegic patients every two to four hours to prevent bed sores.

Sometimes special medical equipment was needed. Multiple amputations and spinal injuries were not uncommon. Chief Nurse Burke noted that, at one point, there were eight paraplegic patients at one time.

Patients with spinal cord injuries or paralysis had to be turned without jarring their spines to one of two positions: lying face up or face down. Stryker frames were used to place them in either position and were designed so that one person could turn a paralyzed patient.[32] HMSC John McCloskey explains the significance of these frames:

> We had twelve modified Stryker frames for paraplegics and quadriplegics. They had to be turned every two hours, catheterized [and] fecal matter cleaned from their rectums.
>
> When time permitted, we read to them. For quadriplegics, we would put a book where he could read it when he was turned on his stomach. Of course, the pages had to be turned and we did that.
>
> Stryker frames were precious pieces of equipment. When patients were transferred to Hawaii, corpsmen from the ward were assigned to accompany them. From Hawaii the patients were sent to a military hospital closest to their home. It was important that corpsmen accompanied these patients. For one thing, they were familiar with operating the Stryker frame. For another, they were responsible for bringing the frames back to Yokosuka.

Japanese Nationals

Stryker frames were nearly impossible to get. Chief Nurse Burke and the doctors had to look to alternative means of procurement.

> One of the medical officers obtained photographs and the specifications for Stryker frames. The Japanese workers in the base ship repair facility constructed these frames.[33]

With her height just under five feet, Lt. Carola Braun (Grandilone), Nurse Corps, U.S. Navy, fondly remembers the Japanese.

> I think they liked me. I was closer to their size. They used to call me "skoshi-san." Skoshi in Japanese means "a little bit."

After having his right arm amputated aboard the *Consolation,* Pfc Herbert Luster, USMC (Ret), was sent to Naval Hospital Yokosuka.

> *A Japanese barber gave me my first hair cut in Yokosuka. He was very kind. He gave me a book to try to help me learn a little Japanese.*

S. Sgt. James Libonati, USMC (Ret), still has the charcoal sketch that a young Japanese man drew of him while he was confined in the hospital in Yokosuka.

> *The Japanese who worked in the wards would come and talk to us. Later as we recovered, we included them in some of our picnics.*

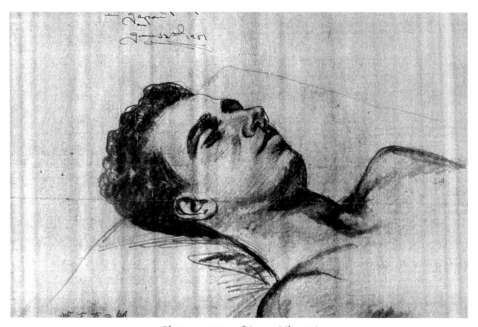

Photo courtesy of James Libonati

S.Sgt. James Libonati, USMC (Ret), was sketched by T. Araki during his stay at Naval Hospital Yokosuka.

Joining the Marine Corps at age sixteen, Cpl. Robert Goode, USMC (Ret), sustained a bullet wound and was at Naval Hospital Yokosuka from October to December 1950.

> *I was not ambulatory because I had a body cast. Because I had a body cast, I couldn't cut the food on my plate. I remember that an ex-World War II Japanese soldier who worked in the hospital came at meal times to cut my food and help me eat. He didn't have to; it wasn't his job.*

Japanese civilians augmented the navy nursing staff. Japanese practical nurses worked beside the navy nurses. Somehow they were able to communicate in their broken English.

Nurses' Quarters

When nurses began arriving in Yokosuka in late August and early September 1950, they were placed in whatever housing was available at the time. The nurses who arrived in early fall 1950 were placed in better dependent housing.

Nurses who arrived sometime in December were placed anywhere there was room. Some were even temporarily placed in warehouses. By the early spring of 1951, about 200 nurses were stationed at Naval Hospital Yokosuka. Conversion of former dependent quarters into hospital wards was completed. New and renovated nurses' quarters were ready for occupancy. Moving day came in the form of a truck that took the nurses from temporary quarters to their new quarters in Buildings E-5, E-6 and E-9.[34]

Photo courtesy of Marilyn Ewing Affleck
Nurses at Naval Hospital Yokosuka were trucked from temporary quarters to permanent nurses' quarters in 1951.

Living in the nurses' quarters gave the nurses a sense of family. Some of the junior nurses shared rooms with bunk beds. Senior nurses often had their own rooms. Yokosuka was beginning to be more like home. Working together and enjoying social and recreational activities created a strong bond among the nurses that cemented lifelong friendships. Nurses during the Korean War were very supportive of each other. "We stuck together. We helped each other out."

The nurses came from a vast variety of backgrounds and experiences and

Photo courtesy of Navy Bureau of Medicine and Surgery Archives (BUMED)
One of the three nurses' quarters at Naval Hospital Yokosuka.

had courageous hearts, gentle spirits, and adventurous souls. Each felt a deep sense of loyalty to country and compassion for others. They all made the commitment to our nation.

They came from all regions of the country: the wilds of West Virginia; the humid cotton fields of Oklahoma; the lights of New York City; the fertile, windswept Midwest; the lake rich North Central; and the seacoast of California. They joined the navy with one goal in mind, to use their nursing skills to help their country.

Through the course of the Korean War these nurses cycled back to Yokosuka, Japan. Some were stationed at Naval Hospital Yokosuka, others served aboard the hospital ships, *Consolation, Repose,* and *Haven,* and came into port periodically.

A rich diversity

Over three thousand nurses served in the Korean War. They came from diverse family and environmental backgrounds yet all had the common goal of being a professional nurse. Five of these nurses served together in Yokosuka when the big surge of patients arrived at the hospital in December 1950.

Photo courtesy of Marilyn Ewing Affleck
From the age of thirteen Ewing intended to be a navy nurse.

Marilyn Ewing (Affleck) was the second oldest of five children. She was "born and raised in West-By-God-Virginia!"

Mom decided to become a nurse and left her home on a motorcycle to train in East Liverpool, Ohio. She met my father, Robert Clayton Ewing, when he had his appendix out. The operation cost twenty dollars.

My dad was a farmer and Mom was a nurse. To make ends meet, they had a small farm and raised dairy cows and chickens.

Mom's sister lived in Maryland. So one summer when I was about thirteen, we drove up to see her. When we passed Bethesda Naval Hospital, I said, "One day I will work here." I did.

I attended the same nursing school as my mom. She graduated in 1919, and I graduated in 1946.

Photo courtesy of James Robert Standing
Inspired by the nurses who cared for her mother, Alexander wanted to become a nurse to help others.

Comdr. Betty Jo Alexander, known to her friends as B.J. or Alex, grew up in Altus, Oklahoma.

I was the youngest of four and picked cotton with my family and learned early that one had to work hard for what one wanted in life. My mother died of a brain tumor when I was six. Maybe that's why I wanted to help people as a nurse.

I participated in the old Cadet Nurse Corps School Program. After completing the program, I decided to join the navy.

My family was not really hip on the idea. My father and brother served in the navy during World War II and had the idea that women were only in the military to be prostitutes. It took a lot of explaining but somehow I convinced them. I entered the Navy Nurse Corps in April 1948.

Photo courtesy of Virginia Jennings Watson
With her parents both World War I navy veterans,
Jennings never doubted that she would join the navy as a nurse.

Redheaded Virginia Miriam Jennings (Watson) grew up in Westchester County, New York. The energy and the pulse of urban living lured her to New York City where she worked as file clerk. Later she joined the Cadet Nurse School Program. After completing the program she decided to join the navy. Jennings father, Allyn, a navy World War II aviator, was thrilled when his daughter decided to join the navy.

Both my mother and father were navy veterans. Mom joined the navy and served as a yeoman (f) during World War I. She was born in Estonia and came to the U.S. when she was sixteen years old. Her proudest moment was when she became a U.S. citizen.

My mother was a woman of few words. Although she never said it, I know she was very proud of my decision to join the navy.

Photo courtesy of Virginia Jennings Watson

Allyn Jennings, proud of his daughter's decision to join the navy, served as a U.S. Navy aviator during World War II.

Photo courtesy of Virginia Jennings Watson

Born in Estonia, Virginia Agnes Greenleaf Jennings served as a U.S. Navy yeoman (f) during World War I. The "f" stood for female.

Growing up near Lake Michigan, Comdr. Jean Ellis (Young) dreamed of being a dress designer. When she realized that the military was experiencing a critical shortage of nurses, she changed her field to nursing.

Photo courtesy of Jean Ellis Young
Ensign Ellis wears the Service Dress White uniform with the flat top that later was changed to what is called "the bucket."

Frederick Fable was a well-known funeral director in Westport, Connecticut. He envisioned his first born, Helen Elizabeth, taking over the family business. For the first nine years of her life, Helen Fable's childhood was uneventful.

At the age of ten I was struck by a truck and sustained a fractured femur. I spent two months in the hospital.
One nurse in particular took very good care of me. She influenced my decision to be a nurse.

The diversity in the nurses' backgrounds added to their ability to resolve medical crises. If a nurse was weighing options to solve an issue, other nurses

Photo courtesy of Helen Fable
Jack Benny arrived in Yokosuka in 1951 with the USO Show. Second from the left, Bobbie Ellis,
Jack Benny and Helen Fable.

offered different perspectives. The diversity in backgrounds became a strength in their team effort. But the binding force that held this team together was their common goals. These goals were their dedication to the nursing profession and their unfaltering belief in the nation and the freedoms it represented.

Social and Recreational Activities

Work hard and play hard were navy traditions instilled early and carried out during the Korean War. During off-duty hours the nurses knew how to take care of themselves. As witnesses to pain, suffering, and death, they celebrated life. When not on duty, they focused on social and recreational activities to take their minds off the tragedies they had seen during intense work.

One of their memorable experiences was climbing Mount Fuji.

Mount Fuji

Photo courtesy of Marilyn Ewing Affleck
We made it! Dr. Norman Christensen, Lt.(jg) Marilyn Ewing, and Dr. Caveness climbed to the top of
Mt. Fuji on 14 July 1951.

Majestic Mount Fuji stands 12,396 feet from base to the top. The "climbers" boarded a local train that rumbled through little Japanese villages and got off the train in Yoshida, where Japanese mountain guides offered their services for about $2.50.[35] Ewing and Jennings both made it to the top.

> *The climb starts out at night. The goal is to see the sun rise on top of Mount Fuji. We both opted for an authentic trip that begins at the foot of the mountain where we rented saddled horses for the first part of the ten-mile journey.*

The Mount Fuji stick is a five-foot wooden pole that is stamped at each of the ten stations along the climb. People who climb Mount Fuji keep their stick to prove that they made the climb.

Ewing made it to Station 10, the top of Mount Fuji.

> *We made it to the top. I was hoping to see the sunrise . . . And see the cities of Tokyo, Yokohama and the surrounding towns. There was nothing but fog, fog and more fog. We couldn't see a thing.*

Then it was time to go back down.

> *The guide forgets to tell you how to get down. You do not climb down Mount Fuji. You can't climb down Mount Fuji from the top. The top is volcanic cinder. You must slide down to Station 6 and then continue the rest of the way on horseback.*

Christmas in Japan

Photo courtesy of Marilyn Ewing Affleck
With the huge influx of patients, Christmas 1950 was quiet, but Christmas 1951 was more festive. Decorations emphasized PEACE.

One of the most difficult sacrifices military personnel make is spending Christmas away from home. This is when the military becomes family. Everyone is in the same situation. Christmas now becomes a collection of combined traditions. Each does his or her part based on Christmases past to create a Christmas present in a strange place. Jennings' first Christmas away from New York was spent in Yokosuka.

> *We were all far away from home. It was getting close to Christmas. I can remember decorating the mess hall and the wards. I bought silk scarves in town to make the ward look colorful . . . festive.*

According to the nurses, the corpsmen made Christmas with creative decorations for the hospital and wards. Jennings recalls:

> *The corpsmen made Christmas trees out of cardboard. The ornaments were made out of cotton balls [and] gauze bandages [and dyed] them red with Mercurochrome. We made little Santa Clauses and put them on each patient's tray.*

Jennings and Ewing both explained that Christmas 1950 was quiet. It was low key due to the incredibly heavy patient load. But Christmas 1951 was more festive. Nurses dressed in Japanese kimonos, had a professional photographer take their pictures and made them into Christmas cards to send home: "Merry Christmas from Japan."

Pfc Rendon, USMC, remembers Christmas at Naval Hospital Yokosuka.

> *I remember Christmas 1951. The ward was decorated. Everyone was happy. The nurses gave all the patients lots of presents. It was a different world from where I came from. The nurses and corpsmen did not have to do this. But they did. I still recall this clearly. The nurses and corpsmen came over all the time . . . to see you . . . talk to you . . . Trying to do things for you. I guess that was better than the Rx. They kept us alive and happy.*

One haunting memory Ewing carries is of a marine patient. U.S. companies sent small gifts to military members overseas, usually little ditty bags with items like shaving gear, cigarettes, combs, and perhaps a deck of cards.

> *I was working late on Christmas Eve. I was really in the spirit so I handed each of my patients the Christmas gifts and wished them a Merry Christmas.*

I approached one young marine. Smiled, gave him my Christmas greeting, looked into his eyes and realized that he had lost both arms. I was stunned. I didn't know what to do, so I just put the gift on his bedside table. He smiled gently and said, "Merry Christmas." I was speechless.

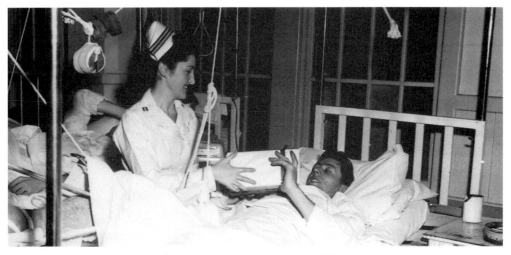

Photo courtesy Carola Braun Grandilone
After World War II, Braun became a navy reservist and was stationed at Brooklyn Navy Yard.
She was called back to serve in September 1950 after the Korean War broke out. Here she is delivering
a Christmas gift from the Red Cross.

Lasting Friendships

The navy nurses enjoyed Yokosuka and Team Yokosuka was great. Jennings took her last tour of Tokyo with her fellow nurses, was energized to be with them, to see Tokyo together. But it was to be the last time. She was going home. Her tour was being cut short although she loved Yokosuka and wanted to stay.

I developed this mysterious allergy that manifested in giant hives that made my lower lip swell and hang down like a Ubangi's. The doctors didn't know what it was. The swelling went into my throat and that was it; they told me I had to be treated in the States. It just killed me to leave Japan.

It was 16 October 1950. Navy nurses Connie Riggs and Ewing accompanied Jennings to the Piedmont Pier where the hospital ship *Haven* was tied up. Jennings would be on her way home aboard the Haven where she was admitted as a patient. She bade her friends a tearful goodbye and waved from the quarterdeck as the ship pulled out. Ewing and Riggs waved.

Photo courtesy Virginia Jennings Watson
Navy nurses Connie Riggs, Ewing, and Jennings (left to right) at the Piedmont Pier in Yokosuka, bidding farewell to Jennings. October 1951.

On 23 October 1999, forty-eight years, almost to the week, Jennings and Ewing met again to share their photo albums and fond memories of their tour. Briefly it was "Home Sweet Yokosuka" when navy shipmates resumed where they left off at Piedmont Pier.

Photo courtesy of Marilyn Ewing Affleck
Ewing Affleck and Jennings (Watson) (left to right) see each other after forty-eight years. October 1999.

Photo courtesy of Jean Ellis Young

A marine sergeant and former patient offered to teach the nurses how to handle weapons.
Ellis (foreground) and Ewing (next to Ellis) practice their marksmanship

Photo courtesy of Agnes Sarna Renner

When the patient load subsided, nurses joined the Yokosuka Women's Softball League.
Sarna is front row, second from the left.

Photo courtesy of Joan Heath Steyn

Lt.(jg) Heath served in Guam before arriving at Naval Hospital Yokosuka in 1953.

Photo courtesy of Joan Tyrell Arcand

Lt.(jg) Joan Tyrell is on duty at Naval Hospital Yokosuka in 1953.

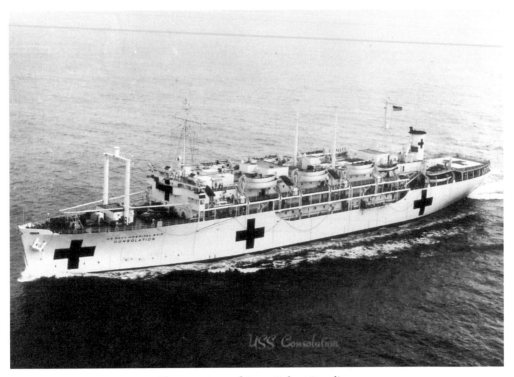

Photo courtesy of James Robert Standing

Consolation, first hospital ship to arrive in Korean waters, October 1950.

6

USS Consolation (AH-15)

I was an infantry platoon leader, Fox Company, Second Battalion. We landed in the afternoon of 15 September 1950 near Inchon and advanced toward Seoul.

I was wounded in the neck and shoulder on the afternoon of 19 September 1950 and evacuated back to Inchon to a field hospital. The next day we were taken to the Consolation in the harbor in Inchon.

I was on the Consolation for about four days. The nurses I remember tended to the sick and wounded in a most professional manner. We all thought very highly of them. They made time to just sit and chat . . . tell a few jokes. They were so selfless and caring that we knew we had the best of care. Our nurses were our rock to lean on.

Maj. Robert Maiden, USMC (Ret)

Departing from San Francisco, California, in July 1950, the *Consolation* was a ship of firsts.[36] She was the first hospital ship to:

• Arrive in Korean waters,
• Include a woman medical officer (doctor) on her staff,
• Use an electroencephalograph (brain wave tracing) machine at sea,
• Install and use a blood bank as standard equipment,
• Mount a helicopter flight deck on the ship,
• Receive casualties from battlefield via helicopter.

The *Consolation* furnished medical support for United Nations Forces and had the capacity to provide medical and surgical care to 786 bed patients.[37]

Photo courtesy of Navy Bureau of Medicine and Surgery Archives (BUMED)
Navy nurses of the *Consolation* with Captains McElroy and Ryan. (Left to right) Lt.(jg) L. Tarvin;
Lt. H. Estabrook; Lt.(jg) D. Watt; Lt.(jg) Floy Mangold; Lt. M.J. Beidelschies; Lt. A. Horner; Lt. G. Welsh;
Lt. E. Bauer; Lt.(jg) J. Bartlem; Lt. L. Williams; Lt. E. Fowler; Lt. A. Pintar; Lt.(jg) Fields; Lt. E. O'Malley;
Capt. J.W. McElroy; Lt. R. Mallen; Capt. C.M. Ryan; Lt. R. Thomas; Lt. C. Ellerbusch; Lt.(jg) A. Wagner;
Lt. H. McBride; Lt.(jg) Toops; Lt. Marion Haire; Lt.(jg) Marie Dalton; Lt. M. Weden; Lt.(jg) E. Vlozaz;
Lt.(jg) E. Norris; Lt.(jg) B. Gregorio; Lt.(jg) F. Jacobson; and Lt.(jg) Helen Brooks.

They Came to Serve

Capt. Helen Louise Brooks, Nurse Corps, U.S. Navy (Ret), celebrated her eighty-first birthday in 1999.

> *From as far back as I can remember, I said I was going to be a navy nurse. I didn't know at that time if the navy had nurses.*
>
> *I completed St. John's Hospital School of Nursing, worked for a while, then joined the navy in 1944. I served until 1946 and then went into the inactive naval reserve.*
>
> *I graduated from Boston University, then went to Yale where I earned my degree in nursing education. In 1950, I volunteered to go back into the navy [because] they desperately needed help in Korea.*
>
> *It took about three weeks to get to the ship.*

Comdr. Marion Barbara Haire, Nurse Corps, U.S. Navy (Ret), grew up about forty miles from Fargo, North Dakota.

I graduated from the Saint Francis School of Nursing and joined the navy in 1943. There was a war; it was the thing to do.

Haire served from July 1943 until July 1946 when she joined the inactive navy reserves and then was recalled to active duty in July 1950. On 30 August 1950, Haire, Brooks and five other nurses received orders to the *Consolation*. They reported to the Federal Building in San Francisco on 14 September 1950, flew from Alameda Naval Air Base on 19 September 1950. This began their journey to the Far East to meet their ship. Haire recounts this trip in her journal.

We left Barbers Point on a DC-4 about 1400 [2:00 PM] . . . an oil leak was discovered on one wing. We returned to have it fixed . . . nothing serious, but rather unsettling. [We] thought of the eleven nurses lost off Kwajalein the day before.

Photo courtesy of Marion Haire
Barber Point, Hawaii. Nurses on their way to the *Consolation*: (left to right) June Bartlem, Harriet Estabrook, Alice Horner, Edna Bauer, Helen Brooks, Marion Haire.

Finally they arrived in Tokyo at Haneda Airport.

After the usual delay, they got us all in a rickety old bus [and] we set out for Yokosuka about forty miles [away].

Once at Yokosuka, they were taken to a deserted building. The nurses were urgently needed aboard ship, so they would be flown to Sasebo. The other officers who arrived with them would take the train. The nurses arrived at Tachikawa Air Base, but the army was not expecting them. They were put up for the night and told that details would be worked out in the morning. One of Haire's bags was lost, so she and Brooks pulled together some nightclothes. It was cold that night. They woke at five the next morning to continue on to Sasebo.

> *We were sent to the terminal to await our plane . . . regulations required everyone flying in an army plane wear parachutes . . . our [slacks] were in our footlockers. After a great deal of discussion, a major waived the rule.*

The six nurses were packed into a C-46 with troops in full combat gear. When they finally arrived at Ashiya, another army base, again the army didn't know what to do with the women.

Finally the army decided the quickest way to get the nurses to Sasebo was by train. After a few stops, the doors opened and the officers they had parted from three days prior in Yokosuka got on the train. The officers made the trip just as fast to this point as the nurses who had flown. When they reached Sasebo, they found themselves in another holding pattern. Haire explains:

> *. . . two weeks after we arrived, we were told that we were to go to Itazuki . . . [then] flown to Kimpo, near Inchon.*
>
> *A few hours before we were to leave, we got word that the ship was on its way back to Yokosuka. We took the train to Itazuki, spent the night. . . . Next day in the rain, [we] took off by air for Haneda Airport. We spent the next two nights and a day in Tokyo lodged at a women's hotel.*
>
> *On the afternoon of the second day we took the train to Yokosuka and as we drew into the station I saw our great white ship! It was Friday the thirteenth and after our weary wanderings, she looked like home. We were ready to begin our life at sea.*

Finally on 18 October 1950, Brooks, Haire and the five other nurses were settled on board. The *Consolation* headed for Wonsan, on the east coast of Korea.

Comdr. Fred Ewing Smith, Medical Service Corps, U.S. Navy (Ret), served as a first class hospital corpsman during the Korean War.

> *I was born and raised in Louisiana. Patriotism, I think, was an important part of our lives. World War II was a popular war, if there is such a thing, and we felt we needed to do something for our country. All the guys in my high school . . . joined the service after graduation. . . . I think in those days, people talked more if you didn't go.*

So I went to the navy recruiting office and said, "Here I am." I was too skinny. The [recruiter] told me to go home and to eat a lot of bananas and drink water. When I went back, I was sick of bananas. They weighed me and I weighed enough, so I got in. . . . I got orders to the Consolation right after the war broke out.

Lt. Floy Mangold (Christopher), Navy Nurse Corps, U.S. Navy (Ret), was stationed at Patuxant River Naval Air Base when she got her orders.

When we received our orders, we were thrilled and excited. We would go home for about two weeks, then we'd go to California to meet the ship.

I went home to Oklahoma, then flew on to San Francisco. Most of the [older] nurses had served in World War II. I was one of the youngest nurses. We were too young and naive to be scared. We worked very hard. I mean we worked night and day around the clock because the wounded just kept coming.

From September 1950 to September 1952, the *Consolation* rendered service to key battles, including the invasion of Inchon and the evacuation of Hungnam. During this period 12,000 patients were admitted to the hospital. About 17,000 were treated as outpatients. Many patients were women and children who were casualties of war.[38]

Patients Arrive

On 19 October 1950, the *Consolation* arrived in Korean waters. Then Comdr. Fred Smith describes their arrival into Pusan.

We pulled into Pusan. The patients on stretchers were waiting for us. I understood some were wounded a week or so earlier. Their bandages were only changed once or twice. There were just too many of them and not enough people or supplies.

So the first night we got about 300 patients. They arrived until about two or three o'clock in the morning. They were lined up on the pier at Pusan. We were using the litter hoists to get the patients onboard. We dropped a hook down to the pier. Those on the pier would hook the stretcher on. It would be brought up to the level of the ship. Then it would be swung on board.

There was a triage officer and nurses right there. They'd look at the patients and tell us which ward to take them to. From then on, it was busy . . . very exciting . . . and pretty tiring as I remember it.

Photo courtesy of Helen Brooks
Pusan, Korea: Wounded arrived by train from the north.

Haire and some of the nurses had a chance to see Pusan. Haire described what she saw:

> We inspected the main street of Pusan . . . there was very little to see, just filth and squalor. Living conditions seem worse than in Japan. The children are cute though. Some of the women dress in curious empire-style dress: an extremely high waistline and a full skirt to mid calf. Sometimes the skirt is separate from the top. Others wear very full pantaloons with a band round the ankle. I don't know how they manage to look so good in them; much better than we [did] in our slacks.
>
> A few of the older men wore their curious white costumes. Though gray would be a better word. A few native articles, mostly brass, were for sale but the prices were exorbitant [and] have tripled since the ship was here last. My corpsmen tell me that beer costs a dollar a can on the black market.

Lt. Comdr. Marie Dalton (Thomas), Navy Nurse Corps, U.S. Navy (Ret), gave her impressions of Korea:

> The first thing you noticed was the smell of the honey pots. And of course, they made kimchee [fermented cabbage]. They didn't diaper their children; [the children] just went in the fields. So of course you'd get those odors.

Photo courtesy of Helen Brooks
Poverty and the lack of sanitation were evident in Pusan.

The marines landed at Wonson and met little or no opposition. On 27 October 1950, the *Consolation* was anchored in Area George, Berth 101, Wonsan Harbor, Korea. Land mines were the main concern. Commander Haire wrote in her journal:

> *The area which is supposedly swept of mines is marked with flags. There are a number of mine sweepers . . . other ships we passed – the Missouri, the Eldorado, the Toledo and several others.*
>
> *Just before noon the patients began to arrive. I had ten by 1500 (3:00 PM). Only two were battle casualties. Both marines with shrapnel wounds. It was satisfying to be busy.*

Still in Wonsan Harbor, the patients continued to arrive. On 28 October 1950, 141 patients were admitted in addition to the 202 already on board.[39] In a journal entry, Commander Haire described the patients arriving.

> *The ward is filling fast and we are kept busy. At 2000 [8:00 PM] we went out to watch patients being brought aboard. A destroyer converted into a transport came along side. Ambulatory patients are brought aboard in a*

chair swung over the side. Litter patients are brought on with a hoist: four lines are fastened to the litter, one on each corner and then the hoist and the pulley brings them up. It's quite a sight. Everything quiet and efficient until all the patients are transferred, and then the sailors from either ship start kidding each other.

Photo courtesy of Helen Brooks
Firing the fining line to the USS *Eugene Greene* (DD-711) to bring patients aboard the *Consolation* while at sea.

Commander Smith remembers the feverish pace.

We got the most serious cases. A lot of abdominal and head wounds. We had great surgeons. The laboratories, the x-rays, and the ORs worked at a frantic pace. The nurses were trying to get the patients cleaned up and comfortable.

We always tried our best to have the best food we could get for them. The kitchen was going all the time. It was teamwork . . . really great to see it happen.

Captain Brooks was a surgical nurse. The operating rooms were definitely kept busy.

We had three operating rooms and at least two operating tables in each room. Sometimes things would be done outside on the stretchers. The patients were brought down according to severity.

We really didn't have a triage. We sort of did the triage outside the operating rooms. It worked. We just didn't have the space.

I remember one smallpox case. I had never seen smallpox before. It was a sight to behold. He was completely covered, including in[side] his mouth and down his throat.

We had a good number of the Korean marines. They were very good patients . . . very stoic people. Many had belly wounds, gun shot wounds or shrapnel. We also had prisoners of war.

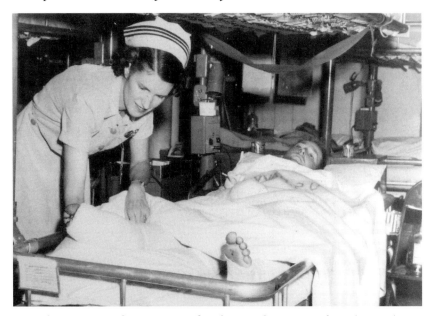

Photo courtesy of Navy Bureau of Medicine and Surgery Archives (BUMED)
Nurse aboard the *Consolation* ensures that the patient is resting comfortably.

The relaxed atmosphere was short lived. According to Commander Haire's journal, more patients arrived on 2 November 1950.

A large influx of marines this afternoon, most of them from a group that [was] ambushed about six miles from Wonsan this morning. All was chaos; it just isn't possible to get everything done. One kid had a bad abdominal wound. They came in unshaven, dirty, exhausted, looking about forty years old. And most of them are still in their teens. I could just sit down and cry for them, if I had the time.

The food situation is a mess. No pun intended. But they think it is wonderful and only complain that it is hard to start eating after having been on c-rations so long.

3 November 1950. This was the worst day yet . . . It is just killing me not to be able to do what one ought for these kids, but there isn't time. Oh well, guess I will go to the movies and [try to] forget my troubles.

4 November 1950. I live from one crisis to another, and it is 3:30 PM before I know it. I go off duty utterly exhausted both physically and mentally. Both a duty and evacuation party is going out tomorrow and so we must brace ourselves for a fresh onslaught of casualties.

7 November 1950. What a night! I never stopped running, except for fifteen minutes for dinner. We had ten to nineteen admissions on C-4 alone. It seems that some sixty Americans met up with a large group of North Koreans and these were the survivors. Things couldn't have been any worse. They came in a steady stream . . . In shock or next to it. Bloody, dirty and all the rest . . . these fellows just don't complain. Although two were critical and two serious, we didn't lose them.

9 November 1950. The doctor told one of my boys [patient], aged twenty, that he would have to lose his right arm. He was running a high temp, so I tried to combine a few words of comfort with an alcohol rub. But if there is a formula that covers such situations, I haven't found it . . . I feel that I failed miserably.

10 November 1950. Today I hit the jackpot, five letters. Now I can understand why even the fellows I met just casually used to beg for letters. Mail becomes so terribly important.

We are running out of supplies and we leave to go back to Yokosuka. We will be in the states by 19 December 1950 and be in Norfolk by 29 December 1950.

18 December 1950. It is below zero on deck. . . . Was out on deck twice to watch the firing which was so loud during the movie that the ship shuddered with it. Star shells, flares, tracers. I am learning a new vocabulary.

23 December 1950. We four nurses on C-3 and C-4 are making Christmas stockings for the boys. It seemed a better idea than giving money. We are making them out of crinoline and stitching them with red yarn . . . filling them with shorts, skivvy shirts, candy, gum, cookies, cigarettes.

26 December 1950. Morale is very high. We left Pusan at noon. The sun shining brightly and the weather mild.

28 December 1950. Arrived in Yokosuka about 4:00 PM [1600]. After dinner we got into our blues the first time in two months. Went over to the club and were swept into a party that a task force was throwing.

> *29 December 1950. The experts think that Yokosuka will be bombed and are making plans accordingly.*

After spending time in Japan for rest and rehabilitation, the *Consolation* reported back to Pusan in January 1951. On 2 February 1951 she remained in Pusan with 648 patients onboard. By March 1951 the *Consolation* was headed back to Yokosuka.[40] Commander Haire wrote in her journal.

> *9 March 1951. Marie Dalton is coming aboard for duty. Its seems amazing, but I hope she will be happy.*

Lt. Comdr. Marie Dalton (Thomas), Nurse Corps, USN (Ret), was born into a navy family.

> *I had five cousins who were in the navy during World War II. My grandfather was a World War I navy veteran.*
>
> *As a nurse, I felt that it was important to take care of the wounded. That's why I joined the navy. I was at Naval Hospital Yokosuka from September 1950 until March 1951.*
>
> *In March 1951, I got orders to the Consolation to replace one of the nurses who got seasick. I packed my seabag and my footlocker. The Consolation was in port in Yokosuka, so I got in a small boat and went to where she was tied up. She just pulled away from the pier. At first they were not going to let me on. They were in the process of deploying. I had papers in hand. Waving them, I explained I had orders to board. They finally let me onboard.*

In April 1951, the navy's *All Hands Magazine* reported:

> *More than 25,000 patients have been treated on board Consolation . . . during approximately seven months in the Korean theater . . . establishing a record for hospital ships . . .*
>
> *. . . (Better than) ninety-eight percent of all wounded UN fighters treated on board have recovered.*
>
> *Dubbed by the GIs as the "Galloping Ghost of the Korean Coast" because of her eerie night view . . .*
>
> *. . . [W]on . . . her the Battle Efficiency Pennant . . . [took] aboard nearly 2,000 wounded at Pusan . . . [at] Inchon, Consolation handled over 1,000 cases . . . [at] Wonsan . . . treated nearly 1,500 and at Hungnam . . . treated a record-breaking 2,000.[41]*

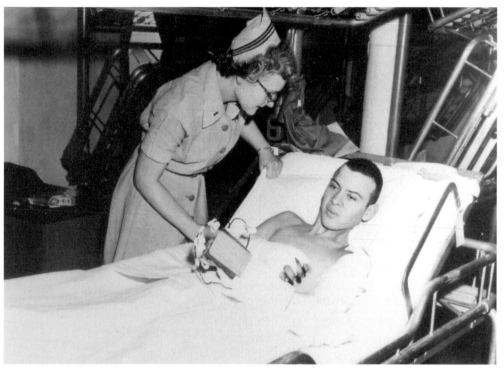

Photo courtesy of Navy Bureau of Medicine and Surgery Archives (BUMED)
Lt.(jg) Muriel E. Ramage supervises Pfc Basillio Renera, USMC, as he does his rehabilitation
finger exercises.

In October 1951, Sgt. John L. Fenwick, USMCR (Ret), was cared for aboard the *Consolation.*

I was wounded for the third time ten days before I was rotated home. I was hit by a North Korean machine gun on 5 October 1951.

Three bullets hit my ammo belt. These were the worst gunshot wounds. They struck me in my left flank involving the iliac crest, three vertebras, destroyed the sacro-iliac joint, severed an artery. I had an exit wound in my lower back the size of a fist.

Platoon corpsman William Snowden saved my life. He dragged me to safety. I was hit by two more bullets in my left upper arm. He was hit twice in his right shoulder. Despite his painful wounds, he dragged me to a safe place and administered to my wounds.

Medevaced to the field hospital, "Easy Med." Was operated on by Lt. Comdr. Phil Cerack. He removed eighteen inches of small intestine. He used a total of 837 sutures during surgery.

Photo courtesy of Navy Bureau of Medicine and Surgery Archives (BUMED)
Navy field medical facilities, "Easy Med," was refuge to injured on the front lines.

After all the surgical tubes were removed, I was flown to the Consolation.

When I arrived there, I thought I was in heaven. Large bunks with clean sheets and navy nurses. My nurse was a lieutenant commander, a World War II veteran. She was wonderful.

She asked me if I would like some ice cream. I couldn't believe it when she asked me what flavor I wanted. I grabbed her hand and kissed it. I said, "You nurses really are angels of mercy." Then I lost it. I cried like a baby slobbering all over her hand. It was hard to believe after a year of suffering deprivations. We were near starvation. There was so much pain and suffering. And now there was something as great as this. This nurse took care of me. It was hard to believe it was true.

Helicopter Deck

According to an excerpt from the 1953 ship's cruise book, the *Consolation* was selected as the experimental hospital ship. It was fitted with a helicopter landing deck. Having a helicopter deck could expedite transportation of the wounded to hospital facilities. In May 1951, the *Consolation* headed back home to California.[42] On the way, Commander Haire received good news and then, as the *Consolation* gets closer to California, Commander Haire reports that the excitement mounts.

28 May 1951. I am getting my back longevity pay.

Approximately $280, which will see me home.

5 June 1951. Our last day out. Tonight we can see the lights of California along the shore and we expect to dock about 2:00 PM tomorrow. Have been picking up radio programs all day; same old commercials. The patients are all excited.

6 June 1951. This was the day. From noon on we lined the rails but the ship was not docked until almost 4:00 PM. There was a navy band. Top brass with brief speeches and crowds of friends and relatives. Very exciting, but hard to realize we are really back in the States.

A sixty-by-sixty-foot landing platform was constructed at the U.S. Naval Shipyard in Long Beach, California. Work was completed on 16 August 1951. The *Consolation* returned to the Korean Theater to resume her mission of medical support. [43]

Photo courtesy of Navy Bureau of Medicine and Surgery Archives (BUMED)
With the new helicopter landing deck in place, patients were flown directly from
the field to the *Consolation*.

Prior to the helicopter landing platform, patients were brought alongside in small boats called LCVPs or LCMs (landing craft). The *Consolation's* electric winch would drop its wire slings into the boats, which would hoist the stretcher (litter) or chair-borne patients aboard. During the typhoon season in the Far East, this operation could be extremely hazardous.

With the helicopter deck in place, the marine helicopters flew their missions of mercy when all small craft at sea were prohibited. A September 1952 article in the *Leatherneck* explained the process.[44]

> *Day and night the Consolation's radio shack picks up messages. Some of them sound like this: "Hospital ship Consolation, this is Charlie Three. I have one walking wounded and two litter cases. One is a serious head injury. Will arrive at your ship in approximately three minutes."*
>
> *Within seconds this message reaches the Officer of the Deck on the bridge. "Flight Quarters" is sounded . . . on the PA system throughout the ship. The chief of medicine is notified. He alerts the neurosurgeon.*
>
> *The helicopter comes in. Hovers over the deck and lands. Before the rotor blades have coasted to a stop, the chock-men have secured the plane in position. The doctor and litter bearers are disembarking the patients. The ambulatory are guided to the hospital spaces. The litters are carried up the ramp to an emergency treatment room for examination and disposition. Total time from shore to ship and treatment, less than five minutes.*
>
> *Capt. John W. McElroy, USN, skipper of the Consolation, has been on hand at most landings to observe and study operations. The Consolation has demonstrated . . . that helicopter flights from the fighting front to a hospital ship are . . . the most practical and fastest method of handling battle casualties.*

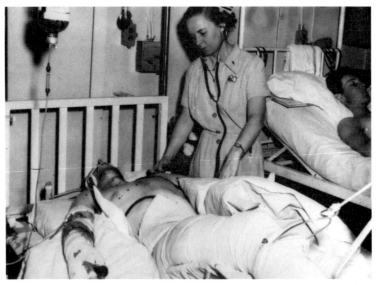

Photo courtesy of Navy Bureau of Medicine and Surgery Archives (BUMED)
Lt. Elizabeth E. Aldrich of Arcadia, California, takes blood pressure of a critically injured patient aboard the *Consolation.*

The *1953 Consolation Cruise Book* provided a synopsis of the *Consolation's* service during the Korean War.[45] In late March 1952, when battle action increased on the Korean western front, the *Consolation* was ordered to Inchon Harbor to furnish medical support to the troops. Soon after her arrival the flow of patients began. By boat and helicopter they came. Battle casualties were admitted and received within minutes of being wounded.

The *Consolation* maintained a daily patient census of 400 plus for ten weeks. In June 1952, she was ordered home. During this period, she underwent overhaul and maintenance.

On the morning of 8 September 1952, the *Consolation* left her berth at Long Beach, California. She was on her way back to Korea. Her mission was again was to aid the men wounded in the Korean hostilities.

The *Consolation* arrived in Inchon Harbor as another big Communist offensive was underway. During the first four days, the doctors, nurses and corpsmen worked around the clock. They got as little as eight hours sleep during a four-day period. In a twenty-four-hour period, as many as sixty-two helicopters landed on her fantail.

Photo courtesy of Helen Brooks
Ruins in Inchon were evidence that war raged in Korea.

After serving for ten months on her third trip to Korea, the *Consolation* was ordered back to the States. All hands felt proud to have contributed to the United Nations effort. During this ten-month stay overseas, the *Consolation* cared for 3,635 United Nations troops and civilians. Since the outbreak of the Korean War in June 1950, the *Consolation* served thirty-one months in Far Eastern waters. She cared for a grand total of 18,433 patients. On average, seventy-six percent of their hospital beds were regularly used at this time.

I was wounded the night of 23 December 1952. I was treated at a field hospital and then taken to the Consolation on Christmas Day 1952. My wounds consisted of mortar fragments in the hand, arm, neck and in my eye, which was destroyed.

Our platoon corpsman gave me immediate care. When we returned to our MLR [main line of resistance], he put me on a helicopter to the field hospital. The corpsman gave me and the other wounded excellent care in a calm and gentle manner.

At the field hospital I was having trouble breathing. So I was given a tracheotomy. I was transferred to the Consolation.

Since I had a lot of congestion it was necessary to apply suction to keep the tracheotomy tube open. The nurses and corpsmen on the Consolation were always busy with patients in the ward. They kept an eye on me. All I had to do was raise my hand. They would come and clean out the tube. Although it was a rather unpleasant job, they did it cheerfully. They did everything they could to make me comfortable.

After about a week on the Consolation, one of the nurses brought in a Polaroid camera. She took my picture so I could send it to my parents. When I got home they told me how much that picture meant to them.

When it was time for me to leave the Consolation for Yokosuka, I got a set of recycled dungarees. I said my good-byes to the nurses and the corpsmen. One of the nurses gave me a set of her lieutenant junior grade bars. I guess she thought I might get a better seat on the plane if they knew I was an officer. It was very thoughtful of her.

Although that was almost fifty years ago I will never forget the excellent medical care I received from the nurses, doctors, and corpsmen of the U.S. Navy. I wish I could recall the names of those who cared for me [but] I will never forget their cheerful faces and how they helped me get over some rough times.

1st Lt. William Gilwee, USMCR (Ret)

Photo courtesy of Marion Haire
The *Consolation* and *Repose* are tied up together in Pusan where they shared the patient load.

Photo courtesy of Navy Bureau of Medicine and Surgery Archives (BUMED)
The chow line aboard the *Consolation*.

Photo courtesy of Navy Bureau of Medicine and Surgery Archives (BUMED)
USS *Consolation* heads for home.

❧ 7 ❧

USS Repose (AH-16)

The nurses aboard the Repose were like a letter from home, a breath of fresh air, a slice of Mom's apple pie and a cold beer, all rolled into one!
M. Gy. Sgt. Kurt Loewy, USMC (Ret)

Photo courtesy of Navy Bureau of Medicine and Surgery Archives (BUMED)
Operated by the Military Sea Transportation service from 3 September 1949 until 26 August 1950, the *Repose* was officially returned to commissioned naval service on 28 October 1950.

They Came to Serve

Comdr. Lura Jane Emery, Nurse Corps, U.S. Navy (Ret), began her navy career 3 November 1947. She was commissioned in Philadelphia and immediately sent to U.S. Naval Hospital, Newport, Rhode Island.

In 1946 I completed my three-year nursing diploma program. For the next year, I was in charge of the operating rooms at night in Pennsylvania Hospital in Philadelphia.

My nursing school roommate joined the navy. She was an ensign in Portsmouth Naval Hospital. She invited me to Virginia one weekend. I decided to join the navy. I was commissioned 3 November 1947.

Photo courtesy of Lura Jane Emery
Stopping in Hawaii, Emery is on her way to Korean waters aboard the *Repose*.

Lt. Eveline Kittilson (McClean), Nurse Corps, U.S. Navy, known as Kit, always wanted to be a nurse.

Ever since I was in fourth grade, I wanted to be a nurse. I remember making posters for the Poppy Day. All I drew were pictures of nurses. Just wanted to be a nurse, that's all. I never had any other desire.

In 1940, I graduated from Trinity Lutheran Hospital with a nursing diploma. I wanted to do something for my country. I didn't know which service to join.

While I was in nurses' training, I went to [the film] "Anchors Aweigh," starring Dick Powell and Ruby Keeler, who was a nurse on a hospital ship. Quite glamorous. I decided to join the navy.

Since I was born and raised in Minot, North Dakota, it was going to be an experience to see the ocean.

I received the application for the navy. It said that I had to have my tonsils out before submitting the form. I never had tonsillitis in my life, but I had my tonsils out. I was sworn into the navy as an ensign, 6 October 1942.

On 1 August 1950, I received orders to the Repose. It was my most memorable duty. It was also the most exciting and challenging.

Photo courtesy of Navy Bureau of Medicine and Surgery Archives (BUMED)
Kittilson ensures that patient care is well documented.

Getting the Ship Ready

From 3 September 1949 until 26 August 1950, the *Military Sea Transportation Service* operated the *Repose*. On 26 August 1950 she resumed her role as a navy hospital ship.[46] At Hunters Point, Lieutenant Kittilson became aware of the work ahead of them.

> *The ship was reactivated at Hunters Point in San Francisco. We were there a month before sailing. I was assigned to the diet kitchen.*

Commander Emery points out:

> *When we arrived, the maintenance people were onboard . . . trying to fix the electrical, sewer and water lines.*
>
> *I thought the ship was in awful condition. We had a lot of cleaning to do.*

On 2 September 1950 the *Repose* departed San Francisco, bound for Pusan, Korea, via Yokosuka.[47] Commander Emery and Lieutenant Kittilson recalled those first few days at sea:

> *As soon as we got outside of San Francisco we had a sea burial for two men on the Benevolence [who had] requested burial at sea. The Benevolence sank in August, while conducting sea trials near San Francisco. All hands attended the service.*

Pusan, Korea

Arriving in Yokosuka 16 September 1950, the *Repose* was on her way to Pusan. Commander Emery describes getting into Pusan:

> *The night before we got into Pusan we ran into a typhoon. I didn't sleep all night; just rolled from one side of [the] bunk to the other.*

The *Repose* arrived in Pusan on 20 September 1950 and remained until 24 October 1950.[48] Lieutenant Kittilson remembers that day:

> *The army band was on the dock to greet us. It really made us feel welcomed. The North Koreans had pushed through to the Pusan perimeter. Pusan now had over a million people. It was overcrowded . . . filthy and smelly. I cannot describe the situation there. The odor even penetrated our ship.*

Photo courtesy of Lura Jane Emery
Military band greets incoming ships making arrival more festive.

Photo courtesy of Eveline Kittilson McClean
Smells of overcrowded, dirty Pusan permeated the ship.

Patients Arrive

Commander Emery notes there was no time to recuperate from the voyage across the Pacific:

> *We got to Pusan and all hell broke loose . . . when the patients started coming onboard. There was no opportunity for rest . . . for a long time. The operating room supervisor and her staff worked for at least seventy-two hours straight.*

In a letter dated 15 October 1950, Commander Emery described her first three weeks in Pusan:

> *The first week we were here we got about two hours of sleep . . . every twenty-four hours. Now we work from 8:00 AM to 10:00 PM. We are on call for trains or planes that arrive during the night . . . all we do is work and take a few moments for chow.*
>
> *. . . We would have given almost anything for more nurses. Our capacity is thirty and we have fifteen for the entire ship.*

Lieutenant Kittilson also recalls the frantic pace:

> *The patients were sent to us by train. It could take twelve to fourteen hours. The trains started arriving about 1800 (6:00 PM). They continued*

until almost midnight every day. Most of the seriously injured were sent to us. We received anywhere from 100 to 150 patients each night. Their ages ranged from seventeen to twenty years old.

The doctors were operating constantly. They did a lot of emergency surgery. If the patient could travel, we sent him to Japan. We didn't keep them more than three days.

I had never seen patients in such bad shape. They had a leg or arm, sometimes both, blown off. Many had been hit in the face. They were blinded. Some had been shot in the throat. They had terrible swelling to the point where they couldn't breathe or swallow. We had a lot of belly wounds. One guy had his brains blown out. There was every kind of casualty.

Since the patients were taken out of the rice paddies, when we got them, they were dirty. Some had worms. Many had lice. After their wounds were cared for, we cleaned them up. It was the first in months that they slept on clean sheets. They were so appreciative.

Sgt. Maj. Jack Jaunal, USMC (Ret), was one of the patients who made the journey to the *Repose*:

When I awoke, I was in an empty building that was converted into an army hospital.

I rolled my head back and stared at the ceiling. I tried to remember what happened to me. We landed in Pusan on 17 September 1950. The first night was spent on the docks. The next day we went north to Taegue. I got hit on the third night.

I was driving a weapons carrier with communications supplies. I was going to one of our units near Taegue. It was a dark night. All of a sudden there was a flash of light. I didn't remember any noise or anything else.

. . . I started to sit up on the stretcher. I noticed my left arm would not move. It was bandaged. Someone had pinned it across my chest to the right pocket of my uniform . . . I rubbed my free hand through my hair. I felt something tacky. It was blood.

It was late when the medic woke me up. I had missed the evening meal. The patients who could travel by rail were being sent to Pusan. He told me that I would be leaving on a hospital train in a few hours. Pusan would be safer and had better hospital facilities.

The stretcher cases were being carried on the train first. I was stand-

ing with the walking wounded. One of them had shrapnel in his shoulder and arms. He was naked from the waist up. Only his bandage kept him warm from the night chill. I gave him my field jacket. He was worried that I would be charged for it. Someone yelled, "All aboard." We climbed onto the train. I found a seat. I sat down and tried to relax.

For the first time I noticed the hospital tag tied to the front of my uniform. My field jacket must have covered it up. I turned it towards me and tried to read it. All I could make out was that I was in severe shock.

I remembered what a nurse said about my being brought in. It was a South Korean who found me. I could remember very little. I felt no pain. I wondered if and when my wife would find out. It would give her a scare. The train was quiet. Each of us had our own thoughts.

We arrived at Pusan. Medical teams and ambulances were waiting for us. As we got off the train we had to get on a stretcher. We were carried to a central location for processing. The doctors and nurses would look at our tags. They would decide what hospital we would go to. I wanted the Swedish hospital ship . . . all those blue-eyed blond nurses. I was tagged for the hospital ship Repose. "Hell," I thought.

I got to the Repose. A hospital corpsman met me at the gangway. He took me below deck to my ward. In the ward another corpsman took over. He gave me a pair of pajamas. He led me to the washroom. He promised to return in a few minutes. It was almost midnight. I was tired. As I removed my clothes I noticed that I smelled like a rice paddy.

Using my free arm, I removed my boots. I unfastened the safety pin and let my left arm drop free. I could move it a little. I removed my clothing. I was a dirty mess. I entered the shower stall . . . turned on the water. Nice, clean, clear, warm water. I was showering when the corpsman returned. He wasn't too happy about me being in the shower so long.

He helped me remove the bandage and splint from my left arm. My wrist was broken. The shower felt good. After rebandaging my arm, the corpsman took me through the ward to my bunk. It was an upper. He helped me up. He told me that the lower bunks were for the "leg cases."

The clean sheets felt good. I was drifting off to dreamland. I felt a thump on my forehead. I looked into a pair of brown eyes. A voice said, "Open." She was a navy nurse. She placed a thermometer in my mouth. She took my good arm to feel my pulse. I could smell her perfume. Then I fell asleep.

The Repose arrived in Pusan, Korea, 20 September 1950. That was the same day I was injured. I arrived the next day. Must have been among the first patients.

I'll never forget those brown eyes I saw on my first night aboard the Repose.

Even though the medical staff remained busy, Lieutenant Kittilson recalled they were very aware that a war was going on:

The fighting was only twenty air miles away. Sometimes we could hear the guns.

In a letter home, Commander Emery wrote:

I just wish I could show the people in the United States a few of my patients, with their eyes shot out, legs shot off. And others are half dead with abdominal wounds. One of our fellows was a prisoner: he was tied to a tree and had both eyes shot out.

Unless you can actually see this, it is hard to believe. The navy corpsmen [who serve] with the marines are being killed like flies.

Most of our patients are marines. They certainly are happy to get on the ship. Ten minutes after we get them, a doctor has seen them and then they are fed and washed.

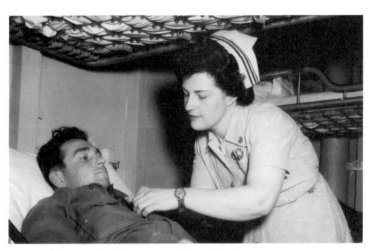

Photo courtesy of Lura Jane Emery

Lt.(jg) Lura Jane Emery makes Sgt. Paul E. Robinson, USMCR, of C Company more comfortable after he received a sniper's bullet in his leg while on patrol in the frigid mountains above Adong.

Some of the patients were covered with body lice. Commander Emery could relate to the lice problem:

Many of the patients that came onboard were covered with body lice. I was cutting the clothes off some of the men who were captured. The body lice were on their clothes and on them. I got the body lice.

It took me three weeks to get rid of those darn body lice. They took all my clothes and put them through the autoclave. I'd sleep on one mattress. Then they'd autoclave or sterilize it. I kept switching bunks. Each time I'd sleep on a mattress, they'd autoclave it.

The lice could drive you crazy. You can feel them crawling . . . all over you.

My ward medical officer told the new patients, "Don't get near that nurse. She's got body lice." The patients would just hoop and howl and have a good time. It was something that relieved the stress.

During the Korean War, medical staff witnessed medical problems they had never seen before. Commander Emery was awed seeing smallpox for the first time:

It was a tremendous experience to care for smallpox patients. We had seven patients with pox, covered from head to feet with pustules. These are small elevations of the cuticle filled with pus.

The patients were isolated. Isolation gowns, gloves and masks were worn by care personnel. Penicillin was probably administered every four hours. I was only a relief nurse. I was only with these patients when their nurse went to chow.

I'll never forget this one sergeant. He was the sickest. He was just one big pustule over his entire body. Unfortunately, we lost a couple of those patients.

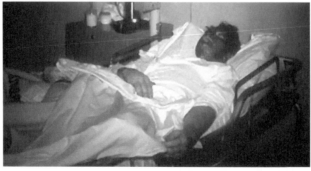

Photo courtesy of Lura Jane Emery
Medical staff saw forms of diseases unfamiliar in the United States.
During the Korean War there were quite a few cases of smallpox.

Seeing the effects of napalm was also an experience for Commander Emery:

> *It was difficult for the doctors to know where to start. They didn't know how to deal with napalm on the skin. It just burns the skin. Burns the tissue.*

When the patient surge subsided somewhat, the nurses were able to go into Pusan. Commander Emery wrote:

> *Pusan . . . it's the dirtiest place I've ever seen. There is no sanitation. They have a ditch along the side of the street that is used as a [toilet]. The odor is terrible.*

During the first year of the war, the *Consolation* was the only hospital ship that had a helicopter deck.[49] The *Repose* would not have a helicopter deck until 25 June 1952. The *Repose* used other means to get patients onboard. The commanding officer of the *Repose*, Capt. E. B. Coyle, MC, USN, explained:

> *The Repose is equipped with eight litter hoists. Two are located on the after part of the main deck. The remaining six are located on the upper deck. Practically all litter patients have been loaded using the single litter hoist. Litters [are then] carried into the forward lobby and classified for hospitalization.*
>
> *At Chinnampo 752 casualties were loaded in forty-eight hours. Litters were loaded using the single hoist on each side of the ship. The lift on the main deck is thirty-seven feet above water. Loading with litter hoists onto the upper deck involves an additional risk; they are located about sixteen feet higher.[50]*

Adm. H. Lamount Pugh, Surgeon General of the Navy, invited a group of medical professionals to the *Repose*. This was an attempt to allow the medical profession to see the unique services of the *Repose*. One of the ship's passengers was J. DeWitt Fox, M.D., editor of *Life and Health* magazine, who described the facilities:

> *Operating rooms were in the middle of the ship. This was where there was the least movement. The operating rooms did not feel the pitch and roll as much. There were operating rooms for general and orthopedic surgery.[51]*

There were x-ray and laboratory facilities. Treatment facilities included whirlpool baths, infrared lamps and diathermy. Each bedside was equipped with a five-station radio dial and placed within easy reach of the patients. Armed Forces Radio would broadcast over these channels. They also listened to church services.

The ship was climate controlled and at least ninety-five percent of the ship was air-conditioned. Ambulatory patients had the run of the sun deck during the day. Dr. Fox called the *Repose* the "Angel of the Orient."

Dr. Fox noted the medical staff's working conditions. [52]

> *Brain injuries, chest wounds and bullet wounds of the abdomen took priority. The doctors had clean gowns and sterile gloves . . . had to scrub their hands in ice-cold water. The entire medical unit went for six seeks without a shower . . . or taking off their [surgical gowns] except for a few hours at a time. Casualties would drift in 200 at a time.*

When casualties arrived at this pace, they were given morphine and a clean dressing that would hold them until they had an opening in the operating room.

On 24 October 1950, the *Repose* departed Pusan with 189 casualties on board that were transferred to Naval Hospital Yokosuka. While in Yokosuka, the *Repose* underwent repairs and maintenance, so the ship's crew and medical staff enjoyed some time off.

Commander Emery wrote about her stay in Japan:

> *Japan is quite the place. It's really beautiful, and I love the people. The army has taken over all the large beautiful resorts and hotels.*
>
> *. . . I went to the Fujiya . . . we had a wonderful time. Lots of good food such as milk, lettuce, tomatoes and even watermelon, which was a real treat.*
>
> *. . . The people are very good to service people, very kind and polite. The nice part of this resort is that it's so inexpensive. The rooms are huge with big windows and beautiful baths and cost fifty cents a day. The food is forty cents per meal. The most you spend for your stay is about five dollars.*

During the second phase of operation, the *Repose* headed for Inchon, departing Yokosuka on 9 November 1950 and arriving 13 November. The next day they sailed for Chinnampo, sixty miles southeast of Pyongyang, the capital of North Korea.

In a two-year review of operations of the *Repose*, dated 2 October 1952, Capt. P.J. Williams, commanding officer, writes:

> *In November 1950 . . . the Chinese Red Forces [entered the war] in support of the North Korean Forces. Their overwhelming numbers forced the U.S. and UN forces to withdraw from advanced positions.*

Photo courtesy of Lura Jane Emery
Chinnampo is located sixty miles southeast of Pyongyang.

With our forces withdrawing from the south, transportation became an issue, which gravely affected the evacuation of casualties, especially from advanced field hospitals. There were many who required immediate hospitalization and continued treatment. Williams continues:

> *Plans were made for a mass evacuation of these casualties. The Repose took 752 aboard at Chinnampo. [The patients] had been brought down by train from Pungyang, loaded aboard the Repose . . . evacuated to Inchon, [and arrived] on 2 December 1950.*
>
> *Without a hospital ship in the area, the evacuation would have been carried out by other vessels . . . not equipped to give the continued care and treatment needed.*
>
> *From this experience, [we learned] that naval hospital ships are an excellent "insurance policy" . . . [when] large [numbers] of casualties . . .*

have to be evacuated from combat areas on short notice . . . . In such emergencies . . . once aboard, treatment is continued until the port of embarkation is reached.[53]

Capt. C. H. Perdue, commanding officer of the *Repose* in *1950* comments.[54]

The most perilous part of the job was the task of steering the ship . . . along the narrow winding channel without running aground.
*   We couldn't use the main channel . . . which was heavily mined. The channel we used was only twenty-six feet deep . . . at high tide [and] the Repose draws twenty-five feet, six inches. We didn't have much water under our keel.*

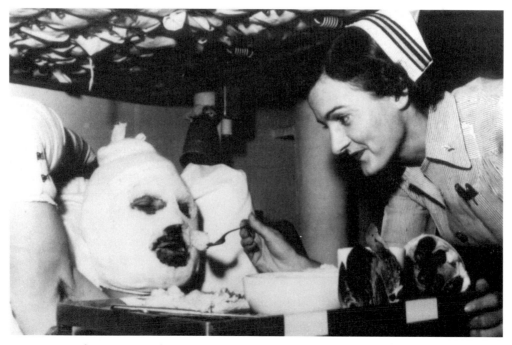

Photo courtesy of Navy Bureau of Medicine and Surgery Archives (BUMED)
Navy nurse feeds a severely injured patient carefully.

As far as he knew, his ship was the largest ever to get though the channel. He added:

The only reconnaissance . . . was a helicopter hovering in front of the ship . . . looking for mines and helping to guide the ship.

The big rescue operation occurred between 28 and 30 November 1950. At that time our ground forces were on the offensive. The mission of the Repose was to provide hospital facilities for our troops in that section.

At the height of the Chinnampo operation, more than 1,300 persons were aboard. It was [a] big problem to feed that many people. But we did. The laundry worked twenty-four hours a day.

Lieutenant Kittilson recalled getting to Chinnampo:

By now, UN forces had pushed the North Koreans up to the Yalu River. General MacArthur said we'd be home for Christmas. Then the Chinese Communists entered the picture.

There was heavy fighting. Most of the injuries were head injuries. Our neurosurgeon, Captain Blood, was sent to North Korea. He assisted the army doctors in the field.

We were anchored at Chinnampo . . . out in the river for about a week. They blackened the ship at night. This is something not usually done to a hospital ship. We had sentries onboard as a precaution in case anything happened.

We were anchored about a week before we received patients. During that time the doctors played volleyball on the deck, and we played cards.

Suddenly the patients started coming. We admitted 780 in three days, filling every bed, including the iron lung. Most were ambulatory. Seriously wounded patients were air evacuated to Japan.

Most of the injuries were shrapnel, a few fractures . . . sumac poisoning . . . frostbite . . . and a few gunshot wounds. The patients told us that the Chinese were well organized. They kept charging . . . regardless of strong [return] gunfire. Some said the Chinese wore metal armor under their clothes. Bullets would just bounce off them. One patient said he hit a Chinese man thirty-nine times with his machine gun. Finally the Chinese man fell.

We transferred 300 patients to the army hospital. These were the patients who would be ready to return to duty.

The *Repose* left Chinnampo and arrived in Inchon, 2 December 1950. For Lieutenant Kittilson, Inchon is another adventure:

We spent the rest of December 1950 anchored at Inchon. There were several other ships there. In early January 1951, the army burned Inchon. It lit up the entire harbor. There were several large oil tanks in flames.

The Rochester, a cruiser, fired several shots on Seoul. We could see the tracers as they left the ship. Several seconds later, we heard the shot. It seemed like the Fourth of July with fireworks. We returned again to Pusan.

Records for the period 8 February 1951 until 30 April 1951 show that the *Repose* spent eighty-two continuous days in Pusan.[55] Total number of patients admitted to the hospital was 3,432. Total patient rations served were 36,102. Average daily admissions to the hospital were forty-two. These totals do not account for outpatient care, which amounted to a correspondingly large number for this period. Repairs were made to the boilers in Pusan without disruption to hospital services.

The *Repose* was in Pusan when the Communist Spring Offensive took place in April 1951, causing heavy casualties to the UN forces. There were other hospital facilities in the area at the time, including two U.S. Army station hospitals, a Swedish hospital ship, as well as the *Jutlandia* (Danish hospital ship). In anticipation of receiving more casualties, the *Repose* departed Pusan with 741 casualties. They headed for Kobe, Japan, where the patients were off-loaded to shore based facilities. They arrived in Kobe on 30 April 1951.

In case the massive influx of patients continued, it would have been possible to evacuate 782 casualties from Pusan to Kobe every five days. This would be accomplished by using one AH-class hospital ship for the evacuation. The recent trip to Kobe was the second time the *Repose* carried out mass casualties within a period of five months. Patient care was uninterrupted during this process.

Gy. Sgt. Robert (Bob) Dion, Sr., USMC [Ret], First Marine Division, remembers his stay on the *Repose*:

In 1951 I was on the Repose for thirty days to recover from leg wounds.

There were not enough hours in a day to complete the nurses' duties [because] there were so many wounded marines and soldiers. Some of the wounded were lying in the passageways, below and above deck.

The nurses all went beyond the call of duty. They were our angels. Seeing them in their clean white starched uniforms reminded us of being home, made us feel good. Their presence meant a lot. Their dedication was great.

It's hard to single out any nurse. They all were great.

Photo courtesy of Lura Jane Emery
The Danish ship, *Jutlandia*, is tied up in Pusan alongside the *Repose*.

M. Gy. Sgt. Kurt Loewy, USMC (Ret), sums it all up. He was on the *Repose* in September 1951:

Ladies, it has been forty-nine years since we met last. Neither you nor I picked the place. I was presented to you on a stretcher. I was dirty, smelly and awake enough to be scared. What I saw was a group of U.S. Navy nurses . . . dazzling in their white uniforms. Smiling and not wasting any time getting patients settled in . . . comfortable and at ease.

I was in pain. My mind was still in the medical evacuation tent. I was on a cot. I was looking at the next tent, the OR, and I saw the growing pile of body parts under a tarp that was not large enough to cover them.

It was finally getting through to me. No more body parts to watch. No more long ambulance rides over Korea's beat up landscape. No more U.S. Army MASH units that would not accept "dirty" marines. No more beat up old gooney bird evacuation planes. I was safe aboard a great ship . . . attended to by expert nurses. I fell asleep. I was home, I felt safe. You have done the Nurse Corps and the U.S. Navy proud. I salute you. I offer you my humble thank you!

By 21 September 1951, the *Repose* had been operating in Korean waters for one year. The *Repose* received a congratulatory message from Vice Adm. C. Turner Joy, commander, Naval Forces Far East, and Gen. James A. Van Fleet, commanding general, Eighth Army.[56]

> *During her year in Korean waters, the Repose cared for 9,487 wounded United Nations' troops. Due to the outstanding performances of the twenty-five doctors, thirty nurses and 199 hospital corpsmen, the mortality rate of the wounded was as low as 3.37 per 1,000 patients.*
>
> *In numerous cases, the most complicated and delicate operations were performed within a few hours after wounds had been incurred. [This] account[ed] in great measure for the remarkable percentage of recoveries among the wounded in the Korean conflict.*

On 7 October 1951, the *Repose* was headed back to Japan. Transferring 140 patients to Naval Hospital Yokosuka was not the only reason for the stop. Commander Emery explains:

> *Jellyfish had clogged our sewer lines. The plumbing . . . the toilets were backed up.*
>
> *As we pulled into Yokosuka, I was later told that they could smell us coming.*

The medical staff and ship's crew was granted ten days of leave. Fresh water and high pressure were used to kill the marine growth and blow out the lines.

The *Repose* remained in Korean waters until January 1952. On 22 January 1952, the *Repose* departed Yokosuka with 221 casualties. She arrived in Pearl Harbor on 2 February 1952 where she took on additional patients and twelve civilian guests of the Secretary of the Navy. While en route to San Diego, the guests of the navy were able to see how a hospital ship operated.

From 15 February 1952 to 6 May 1952, the *Repose* was in Long Beach Naval Shipyard having a helicopter-landing platform installed on the fantail. It extended the full width of the ship with a safety net along the sides.

Before deploying for the Far East, the *Repose* held an open house to commemorate the forty-third anniversary of the Navy Nurse Corps. After riding out a typhoon, the *Repose* arrived in Inchon on 24 June 1952. On 25 June, she received her first patient by helicopter:

Photo courtesy of Navy Bureau of Medicine and Surgery Archives (BUMED)
On 25 June 1952, in Inchon, the *Repose* received her first patient by helicopter.

It was noted that those received by helicopter were more serious casualties . . . indicating that speed and comfort in transporting badly wounded casualties were essential . . . [the] helicopter . . . fulfilled this requirement.

For the first thirty days of operations at Inchon a total of 150 casualties were received by helicopter. [This] represent[ed] seventeen and a half percent of the total number of 855 patients received by boat and helicopter . . . during the first thirty days of operations at Inchon, from 25 June to 25 July 1952 . . . most of the casualties received by helicopter were . . . either serious or critical . . . [and] were taken to surgery as soon as possible.

Many cases arrived receiving blood and/or oxygen in flight. A container of blood was strapped to the side of the helicopter with a needle taped to the patient's vein . . . a continuous flow of blood was received in flight. During transfer from the helicopter into the hospital, a bottle-carrying rack . . . slips over the litter handles so a continuous flow of blood is assured. . . . The average time for admission to the hospital from the helicopter deck was about two minutes.

The types of wounds that were considered serious or critical were head, chest and abdominal wounds. Others included traumatic amputations of arm[s] and leg[s].

Out of a total of 855 patients admitted to [Repose] . . . for the first thirty-day period of operations at Inchon, 150 were received by helicopter . . . 705 were received by boat.

It has been stated that if a casualty can survive the first three hours after being wounded . . . his chances of recovery are good provided adequate hospitalization is available within a reasonable limit of time.

It is considered that the installation of a helicopter platform on naval hospital ships represents remarkable advance in care of the sick and wounded . . . [since] landings can be carried out day and night, at an average rate of twelve to fifteen per hour, or at the rate of one every four or five minutes.[57]

As a non-ambulatory patient, Maj. Howard "Joe" Collins, USMCR (Ret), observed the work the nurses performed:

During the Korean War, I was assigned to the 4.2´ Mortar Company [as] a wire man and radio operator. I was assigned with the forward observer.

I was a patient aboard both the Repose and Consolation. This was from 29 October 1952 through November 1952. I was operated on aboard the Repose and at Naval Hospital Yokosuka.

When we asked for a urinal bottle, we either asked for a P-38 or a B-29. Not much meaning to the layman, but it always brought a chuckle from the nurses.

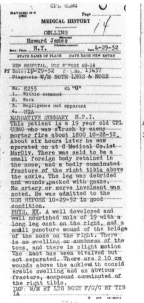

Courtesy of H. J. Collins
Cpl. H. J. Collins' medical records.

Courtesy of H. J. Collins
This tag placed on Cpl. H.J. Collins
assigned him to the *Repose.*

Collins continued:

> *I guess we always noticed the nurses at night. This is a time when the ward is quiet and patients are asleep. It can be a really lonely time for patients. This is the time you can really hear someone in pain or having a nightmare. The nurses were always there for us. Their talking to us always helped.*
>
> *There is no doubt [that] I give the nurses my heartfelt thanks for all they did. They made my final recovery a reality.*
>
> *I still remember the day I was taken off the helicopter [onto] the deck of the Repose. I'll never forget the face of the nurse who bent over my stretcher, took my hand and said, "Hi, Marine." She told me that I was going to be fine. The nurses' care certainly was a contributing factor to my overall recovery . . . both physically and mentally.*

By May 1953, 16,000 patients were treated and cared for aboard the *Repose*. This floating hospital had forty percent of the capacity of Bethesda Naval Hospital or Walter Reed Army Hospital.[58]

Cpl. Jackie L. Kelley, USMC (Ret), was flown to the *Repose*:

> *I boarded the Repose on 6 February 1953 and was met at the flight deck by three doctors, five nurses and corpsmen.*
>
> *During the first ten to fifteen days I had my arms tied to the rack above me. I lost my right hand and the use of my left. Even though they talked of replacing fingers in later years, the doctors of the Repose saved two of my fingers by surgically putting them back on my hand so I had a thumb and two fingers.*
>
> *While I was on the Repose, many nurses and corpsmen talked to me when I couldn't sleep at night. The nights are long on a hospital ship. The nurses and corpsmen made the nights much shorter. They even held a cigarette for me.*
>
> *I never remember a nurse or corpsmen giving a negative look or comment when they had to do the unpleasant task of wiping me or feeding me.*
>
> *I was on the ship until it docked in San Francisco on 6 March 1953.*
>
> *I owe my life to the doctors and nurses of the Repose. I had an eleventh grade education when I was wounded. I now have a wife of forty-five years, three children, a master's degree, was an extremely successful teacher for thirty-eight years. I retired in 1996.*

Photo courtesy of Lura Jane Emery

Full staff of nurses aboard the *Repose* taken in Pusan harbor aboard ship.

Photo courtesy of Lura Jane Emery

Navy nurses aboard the *Repose* in Chinnampo, Korea, located above the thirty-eigthth parallel.

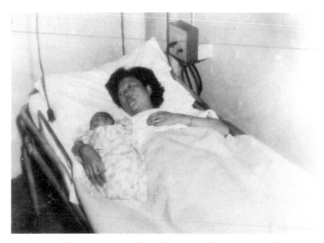

Photo courtesy of Navy Bureau of Medicine and Surgery Archives (BUMED)

Hospital ships anchored in Korean waters treated injured UN soldiers and also assisted with civilian medical care. Daisy Mah was the first baby born aboard the *Repose*.

Photo courtesy of Lura Jane Emery

Christmas 1950 on the *Repose*: Lura Jane Emery (front left corner), Edna Daughtery, Jones, Barbara Heine, Pinky Connors, and Eveline Kittilson (back).

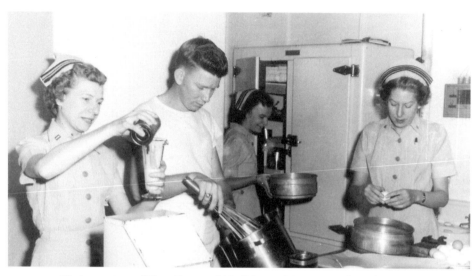

Photo courtesy of Navy Bureau of Medicine and Surgery Archives (BUMED)
Making Christmas fudge for wounded men aboard the *Repose* anchored in Pusan:
(left to right) Lt. B.E. Boumal, George Marshall, Lt.(jg) B. Ellis and Lt. Comdr. Roberta Ohrman.

Photo courtesy of Lura Jane Emery
Capt. Winnie Gibson, NC, USN, director of the Navy Nurse Corps, visited the *Repose*: (left to right)
Rear Admiral Braddus; Captain Gibson; Rear Admiral Pugh; Captain Coyle, medical director, *Repose*.

Photo courtesy of Navy Bureau of Medicine and Surgery Archives (BUMED)

The *Repose* arrived at Inchon on 13 November 1950, then to Chinnampo on 19 November and returned 1 December with 752 casualties from Pyongyang.

❧ **8** ❧

USS Haven (AH-12)

When I first saw the nurses aboard the Haven I thought they were the most beautiful people I had ever seen. At the time, I was in such pain but didn't know the seriousness of my injuries. The nurses immediately made me comfortable and gave me hope that I'd survive. How did you ladies keep these uniform dresses so clean?

Sgt. Nicholas Gervase, USMC (Ret)

Photo courtesy of Navy Bureau of Medicine and Surgery Archives (BUMED)
Haven class ships have eight decks. Three decks are below the waterline. The forward portion of the ship is where the hospital is located.

In an article in the *American Journal of Nursing*, May 1953, Eleanor Harrington describes life "Aboard a Hospital Ship."[59]

Aboard the U.S. hospital ship Haven, the order came clearly over the ship's intercommunication system, "Go to your stations, all to special sea detail." Shortly afterward, the ship backed away from the pier.

When the Korean War broke out, the *Benevolence* was bound for Korea. She was one of the hospital ships that would serve in Korean waters. In preparation, she conducted her sea trials. On 25 August 1950, she collided with a civilian vessel. The *Benevolence* sank 1.89 miles due west of Seal Rock off San Francisco. The *Haven* was taken out of the mothballed fleet, recalled to active duty to replace the *Benevolence*. The *Haven* was recommissioned on 15 September 1950.[60]

Even before deploying she was short-staffed. The minimum number of nurses for a hospital ship of this size was thirty and there were twenty-five nurses on the *Haven:*[61]

Some [of the nurses] were reservists . . . recently recalled to active duty. Sailing on a hospital ship was a new experience for most of them.

Although they all knew their destination, no one . . . spoke of it. They were busy getting acclimated to their new surroundings. Before long they were used to shipboard living . . . acquainted with their shipmates . . . and quite familiar with . . . the nautical terms.

The USS Haven is a floating hospital [that] accommodate[s] 795 patients. Besides the nursing staff, she carries a staff of twenty-five doctors, three Medical Service Corps officers . . . ninety-four hospital corpsmen . . . three dental officers, and six dental corpsmen in addition to the [ship's] crew.

The eighteen wards aboard the ship vary in size from twenty-six to fifty-eight patients. The double-decker bunks have comfortable mattresses . . . the orthopedic wards are equipped with fracture beds . . . [and] have appliances for any necessary traction. Small trays [are] fastened to the bunks. [They] replace the more familiar bedside stands . . . [and] help keep the patients' personal belongings within reach.

It was 3 October 1950. The *Haven* left Pearl Harbor for Yokosuka, Japan:

The day began with the announcement to the crew over the "squawk box," "Reveille, Reveille, all hands heave out and trice up. The smoking lamp is lighted in all authorized spaces." After a hearty breakfast, each corpsman proceeded to his particular job assignment, some to the wards, others to the various clinics.

Ten days later, the *Haven* arrived at U.S. Naval Base Yokosuka. She departed 15 October for a three-day voyage to Inchon, Korea:

> *The Haven arrived at Inchon October 18, 1950, and served as base hospital . . . for six weeks. During that time [she] averaged 530 patients daily . . . normal surgery schedule for each of the ship's thirty-five doctors was twenty cases a day.*
>
> *During the Haven's eighty-day stay at Inchon, only one death was recorded, that of Lee Jae Young, a Korean stevedore. [He was] critically injured while unloading cargo on the SS Marquette Victory.*
> **(8 November 1950, San Francisco Chronicle)**

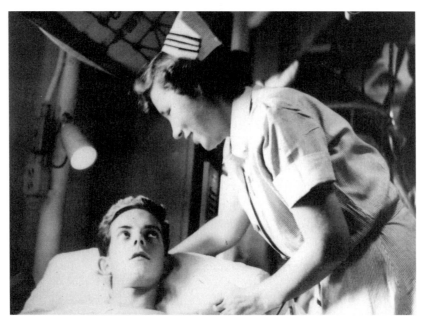

Photo courtesy of Navy Bureau of Medicine and Surgery Archives (BUMED)
Navy nurse straightens pillow of patient in the sick ward of the *Haven*, Inchon, Korea, September 1952.

While the ship was tied to the pier:

> *Patients were received by boats (LSUs, LCMs), hospital trains, and ambulances. A doctor, a nurse and four corpsmen were assigned to each ward. The nurses worked eight-hour watches on rotation . . . being on duty every fourth day. This meant that they must be available when a new group of patients arrived. When many casualties were to be admitted, every one reported back to her duty station. We were forewarned of*

the arrival of patients by announcement, "Litter and embarkation teams, man your stations."

The embarkation officer, [with] a physician, screened the arriving stretcher cases. He evaluated the condition of the patients . . . type of wounds, injuries, or disease. Then determined to which service, ward, and bunk (upper or lower) he was to be assigned. Ambulatory patients were admitted through the Records Office.

As soon as a patient arrived on the ward, the nurse and a corpsman greeted him. The next immediate task was to clean him up. Sometimes this was quite a task . . . especially if the patient had been in his bunker when he was hit. After he had been scrubbed from head to toe . . . he was comfortably tucked between white sheets . . . under the protective care and observation of an ever-attentive nurse, [who] symbolized home to many.

The wounded were usually kept aboard ship approximately three weeks . . . they were transported by plane to hospitals in Japan . . . [then] air-evacuated to the States. Many patients could be returned to their own units directly from the hospital ship.

Many of our patients were Koreans . . . we had to comprehend . . . interpret customs and language strange to all of us. Two names, Lee and Kim, appeared most often on our records.

One Lee, like all patients on admission, received a short haircut . . . a complete bath . . . necessary cleaning of his wounds. At first he was frightened and bitter . . . especially after we had cut his hair. The men he esteemed wore long hair . . . their enemies wore their hair short.

Under the constant care of the nurses and corpsmen Lee's right foot improved . . . he was able to wear a new shoe.

Now that friendship had a place, he improved more rapidly. He even sang as he assisted in caring for other patients. Like many other Korean patients, he shed tears . . . on the day he left the ship.

By November, still at anchor in Inchon, the *Haven* admitted 1,204 patients and discharged 982. The daily average was 536. Only eighteen beds were empty on 19 November due to a high patient census of 778.[62]

The *Haven* remained at anchor in Inchon through December 1950. The total number of patients was kept as low as possible through evacuation of patients to Naval Hospital Yokosuka Japan. Patients who transferred required prolonged hospitalization. During the month of December, 610 patients were admitted and 916 were discharged. The daily average was 217. In addition to the increased workload, there were four air raid alerts on 6, 12, 13, and 20 December. Fortunately, no action took place.

Cpl. E. Boyce Clark, USMC (Ret), was in the Third Replacement Draft that arrived in Pusan, Korea, 1 December 1950:

> [I] received mortar fragments to [my] left arm near the Hwachon Reservoir on 2 June 1951, spent a day or two at a field hospital and then was transferred to the Haven.
>
> The day I'll always remember aboard the Haven was when a nurse came by to give me a bath and shave. We talked about the possibility of my losing an arm. She was most reassuring and comforting. But gangrene had set in and there was nothing the doctors could do but amputate. Several days later, I was transferred to Naval Hospital Yokosuka. I never got the chance to thank her for [her] kindness. I never knew her name.

On the road to recovery, Corporal Clark was thankful for what the nurses aboard the *Haven* and at Naval Hospital Yokosuka did for him:

> Nurses aboard ship and at the hospital were more than helpful. They visited with us, brought us juice and refreshments and helped us with letter writing. As we amputees recovered, it was the nurses' sense of humor that helped boost our spirits.

The navy doctors were clearly also part of this professional medical team. Corporal Clark recalls the first time his dressing had to be removed after his amputation:

> I recall the first time the dressings to my injuries were changed on the Haven. It was most unpleasant as the bandage had dried out and stuck to the wound. I sat on the examining table. The doctor walked in. My first thought was who is this guy and what is he going to do? He explained what he was going to do. He proceeded to soak the dressings with peroxide. He slowly removed the dressings from my arm as well as the graft on my leg. I'll always remember his patience and calm manner.

By January 1951, the Communists were on the offensive and reached the out-
skirts of Seoul, South Korea, during the first few weeks of the month. The stalwart ship, *Haven,* remained anchored at Inchon when UN forces were
retreating south. The city of Inchon was fired on and abandoned by UN forces.
The only UN vessels moored at Inchon Harbor were the *Haven* and three rocket
ships. Finally, after being moored for eighty continuous days in Inchon, the
Haven departed for Pusan, Korea.

Photo courtesy of Navy Bureau of Medicine and Surgery Archives (BUMED)
Two children in Pusan watch the activities as patients are placed on board the *Haven.*

On 8 January 1951, she arrived at Pusan and was anchored at Pier One,
northern entrance. That same day, ninety patients embarked and added to the
155 patients already on board:

> *At first view, Pusan was a conglomeration of rectangular huts clustered
> by the thousands along dirty paths. Koreans squatted impassively in the
> doorways of their dimly lighted huts. This was the place of refuge for
> thousands of Koreans who had been left homeless by the war.*[63]

From Pusan, the ship deployed to Yokohama via the Simonseki and Bungo
channels and did not enter Tokyo Bay until 11 January 1951. Arriving at
Yokohama, she disembarked 150 army patients and was underway once again
for Yokosuka.

The medical staff and ship's crew welcomed nine whole days of rest and recreation in Yokosuka, Japan, from 13 to 19 January 1951. Approximately every three months the *Haven* returned to Japan and the wounded were transferred to the hospital ashore. All personnel were granted a well-earned leave:

In those happy and carefree days we temporally forgot all the tragedies of war. Then it was back to work again.

Photo courtesy of Navy Bureau of Medicine and Surgery Archives (BUMED)

A female Korean dock worker in Pusan looks on as a patient is taken aboard the *Haven*. Hospital ships from Denmark and the United Kingdom are also part of the United Nations Mercy Fleet. 11 June 1951.

Marine 1st Sgt. Andrew Peter Boquet, stricken with infectious hepatitis and jaundice, boarded the *Haven* in March 1951:

My first contact with a navy nurse was on the hospital ship Haven. I was filthy dirty and sick as a dog. This nurse had me bathe and dump my clothing. She gave me clean PJs and put me in a nice clean bunk. She then gave me a tall cold glass of milk. She looked so beautiful in her spotless white uniform. I'll never forget her. Don't know her name.

In April 1951, Chief Nurse Lieutenant Ruth Cohen, *Haven*, was asked by Capt. Winnie Gibson, NC, USN, to assess the contribution of the navy nurses in the war effort. Captain Gibson was the director of the Navy Nurse Corps during the Korean War:[64]

I do not believe that the nurses on a hospital ship make any unusual contributions to medical care. Their nursing skills may be utilized more intensively for certain periods, but they are the same skills and abilities that navy nurses contribute wherever they are on duty.

[N]urses on the Haven have made a contribution to the morale of patients. The patients are sincere in their appreciation of being cared for. Both officers and men of all branches of service have voiced that appreciation sincerely, respectfully, and frequently.

Although it is difficult for me to evaluate our contributions, I find it much easier to evaluate what our duty in the present conflict has done for us. I see the nurses growing in understanding, in [wanting] to be of service . . . [I see them making] adjustments to many peoples and situations. I hope this growth continues.

Gy. Sgt. Donald Mahoney, USMC (Ret), recalls his stay on the *Haven*:

I was wounded in the left leg on Sunday 17 June 1951. I was treated by a navy corpsman and evacuated by helicopter to a navy medical field unit. They removed shrapnel from my leg. I spent the night there in a tent.

The next morning we were put on trucks and taken to a train. From there we went to Pusan, Korea. That's where I boarded the hospital ship Haven. I spent almost a month onboard. The doctors and nurses were great. Had good care and good food.

It's been forty-eight years, and it's hard to remember some things, but I will never forget the care I got from the navy corpsmen, nurses and doctors.

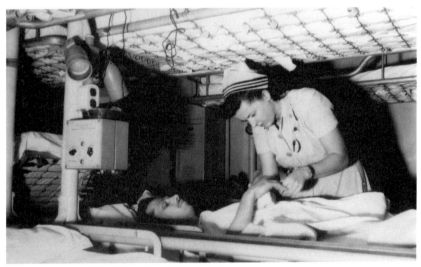

Photo courtesy of Navy Bureau of Medicine and Surgery Archives (BUMED)
Lieutenant Dargitz of California examines the hands of a U.S. Army sergeant aboard the USS *Haven*.

I remember how compassionate the nurses were when the wounded called out in pain. I have the greatest respect for the navy nurses who served during the Korean War.

In October 1951 after having admitted over 8,500 patients and treated an additional 3,000 outpatients, the *Haven* ended her first Korean cruise and set course for home.

On 7 January 1952, the *Haven* began its second Korean cruise that lasted nine months. Operating in Pusan and Inchon, she received patients from the front lines by trains and helicopters. From time to time she returned to Japan to evacuate patients and effect repairs.[65]

When the *Haven* arrived in Pusan, she was greeted by the *Consolation*:

Our sister ship, the Consolation, was waiting for us to relieve her. As we approached, her military band on her flight deck welcomed us with, "If I Knew You Were Coming I'd a Baked a Cake." This became our theme song in Korea.[66]

In November 1952, Hazel Holly, club editor, *San Francisco Examiner*, Women's Department, participated in the navy's guest cruise program. This is where civilians are invited to ride navy ships. She wrote a series of articles about her cruise on the *Haven* entitled "Operation VIP."

In one month from July 23 1952 – August 23 1952, the surgical and medical staff of the Haven handled 1,200 cases. They used as many medical supplies in that month as they normally use in half a year. For three weeks during that period, they never closed . . . the operating rooms, [that were] open twenty-four hours.

From an operations point of view, a hospital ship is a double command. The ship's company runs the ship, so that the hospital can operate.

It took us almost three hours today, just to tour, to walk through, the wards of this hospital ship. On an operating table today [we saw] a boy, whose arms and legs [were] gouged horribly by shrapnel.

This is a repair ship, a repair ship for young Americans.

About 4,667 patients were received and treated, and fifty-four percent of these were subsequently discharged from the ship and returned to full duty. The efficiency and worth of the ship is reflected in the low death rate, only one-half of one percent of all cases handled died.

In August 1952, Sgt. Nicholas Gervase, USMC (Ret), was a corporal and a machine gunner:

I was in the assault on a Chinese outpost half a mile in front of our main lines. I was wounded on 13 August 1952. This hill was what we called Bunker Hill. The Korean name for it was Chang Dan.

We were issued flak jackets in July 1952, and fortunately I was wearing mine that day. A mortar shell landed right next to me and blew in the right side of my chest.

A corpsman held my chest together and kept me alive on Bunker Hill. Who he was is a complete mystery to me. I have no idea what his name was or if he survived this action.

I was carried half a mile through a minefield. My stretcher was placed on a rack in a jeep. The road was so rough I could not make this trip.

The medical personnel flagged an evac helicopter. They transferred me into the wire basket on the outside of the helicopter. This helicopter had a large Plexiglas-type bubble for the pilot. There was a wire basket on each side. I was flown to a field hospital.

It was several days before I was taken to a hospital ship. When my stretcher was carried aboard the Haven and I saw the nurses in their crisp white uniforms, I thought I died and went to heaven. Their very presence made me feel better.

I was in pretty bad physical shape. I had my first and most major operation on the Haven about 20 August 1952.

All of the medical people, doctors, nurses, and corpsmen, were going the extra mile to do their very best to keep me alive and as comfortable as possible.

The ship was maxed out with casualties. On Bunker Hill (Chang Dan) alone we had 313 wounded, in addition to 48 killed. Not all of them were on the Haven but there were a lot of marines who were injured in other actions.

About 2 November 1952, Mrs. Bradner W. Lee, Jr., a member of the National Defense Advisory Committee, was aboard the *Haven*. The *Haven* was in Korean waters.[67]

[T]he nurses on [the Haven], an . . . understaffed hospital ship . . . work[ed] forty-eight hours without rest in a condition bordering anemia. [The nurses were] . . . giving their own blood for [patient] transfusions.

According to current blood bank standards, an average human being has ten to twelve pints of blood. The number of pints of blood is determined by the person's size. During a blood donation, only one pint of blood is taken. It takes about eight weeks before that individual can donate blood again.

Flight Deck

At this time the *Consolation* was the only ship with a flight deck. Due to the creative thinking of the commanding officer of the *Haven*, a makeshift flight deck was created. The deck consisted of two barges moored to port and starboard of the ship:

> *Doctors and nurses had never seen the type of cases they were seeing as a result of the war. One surgeon said, "In World War II, men with injuries like these would have been dead before we ever saw them."*
>
> *Now thanks to helicopter pilots, whole blood and bullet proof vests . . . doctors and nurses aboard have achieved this record: . . . between 23 July 1952 and 23 August 1952, 1,204 patients were admitted to . . . Haven at anchor in Inchon Harbor. Of that number, nine boys died.*

Photo courtesy of Navy Bureau of Medicine and Surgery Archives (BUMED)
Platforms on either side of the *Haven* permit helicopters to land wounded.

Then-Lieutenant Eleanor Harrington, chief nurse, described this flight deck in an article in *The American Journal of Nurses,* May 1953, article:

> *Call to "Flight Quarters" at first was a novelty. But soon it came to mean more to Bunker Hill casualties, our marines. Bunker Hill in Korea*

. . . is located northeast of Panmunjom. [It] derives its name for the elaborate bunker system devised by the Communists.

One morning a wounded man was taken from the flight deck. While leading a squad of men the day before . . . he had been hit by a mortar blast . . . [was] bleeding and dying on Bunker Hill. A navy corpsman found him and stemmed the flow of blood. He was brought by helicopter to our ship.

He was taken immediately to the operating room within a few minutes of his arrival on the ship. The patient, apparently in extreme shock, was still dressed in battle attire . . . Examination revealed severe wounds along his entire right side . . . The arm and leg more severely wounded than the torso because of his bulletproof vest.

Mrs. Lee, NDAC, was impressed with how the makeshift flight deck worked and the efficiency of surgery aboard the *Haven*:

A cleverly established helicopter deck made it possible for wounded men to be picked up on the battlefield and, within thirty minutes, be in surgery.

The flight deck and the strategic location of Inchon were key to getting patients from the battlefield to the hospital ships:

Because of geography, hospital ships can anchor within one half hour's helicopter flying time from the front. This was also made possible because Inchon Harbor remained intact.

Photo courtesy of Navy Bureau of Medicine and Surgery Archives (BUMED)
Marine HRS helicopter lands on pontoon barges anchored alongside the *Haven*.
The ship is in Inchon Harbor.

Mrs. Lee described the conditions on the *Haven*:

Off the coast of the Korean Peninsula, the Repose and the Consolation rotate with the Haven on a six-month basis to care for the wounded [and] deliver them to the U.S.

While the time from battlefield to surgery is without precedent the swiftest, the supply of nurses and blood, unbelievably, is lacking. Add to that the seriousness of the cases that come aboard and you have a picture of terribly overworked doctors, nurses and hospital corpsmen.

There were 329 patients and only twenty-five nurses. A mere minimum of thirty [nurses are] required to do an adequate job. Whole blood can be kept only eight days, and the Haven during this stint had been harbored at Inchon for nine months.

The doctors were getting cases never seen before, either in civilian or military work, and . . . they were actually bringing men back from the dead.

The nurses on the Haven averaged about two hours rest a day, sometimes less. Their only diversion was at Pusan where the only American nightclub, Old Ironsides, is located. There is nothing in Seoul or any of the other cities where the ship docked. It's a somber job. The nurses are the guardian angels of the wounded men. It would help if there were more nurses . . . [so] . . . they didn't have to worry about becoming anemic.

Mrs. Lee described the *Haven*'s arrival in the U.S:

The saddest thing was docking at San Francisco. When the ship was nearing the Bay City, the men who could wear shoes were shining them up to a brightness that dazzled the eyes. As the patients were lined up on stretchers to land, their first return to the States for many long, pain-ridden months, they now peered eagerly for welcomers. There was no band and no happy throng of well wishers; only a handful of apprehensive relatives and somber ambulances.

During the time that Mrs. Lee was on board, the *Haven* received a case they referred to as the "miracle." The patient was William Gentleman, a twenty-one-year-old hospital corpsmen, third class, from Grand Rapids, Michigan. He told the doctor:

The only thing I remember is that we were going up a hill. I was with the marines. I think I remember I was giving someone morphine.

The marines he was with told the doctor on the *Haven* the rest of the story:

> *An eighty-eight-millimeter mortar fragment tore into his left temple, took out his left eye, and passed completely through the front part of his brain. Even after he was hit, he went right on functioning automatically. First he'd treat someone, then he'd pick up a rifle and fire awhile. He kept at it until he rallied the company; then he collapsed.*

The doctors on the *Haven* continued the story:

> *When he came in here he was in a coma. He looked like he ought to be dead; the front part of his head was gone. After a seven-hour "miracle" surgery aboard the Haven, we managed to save his life.*
>
> *A team of navy surgeons performed a frontal lobotomy. The sailor gradually recovered his memory and was considering going back to school after he was discharged from the navy.*

Mrs. Lee recalled injuries sustained by a patient:

> *The man was on the operating table for brain surgery alone for seven and one-half hours. He required thirty-nine pints of blood before he could be called out of danger.*

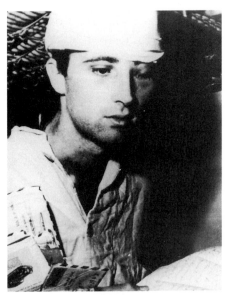

Photo courtesy of Navy Bureau of Medicine and Surgery Archives (BUMED)

Hospital Corpsman Gentleman, the "miracle patient."

In January 1953 the *Haven* was on her way back to Korea. This time with the newly installed flight deck. The flight deck changed operations considerably as the 1953 Cruise Book for the *Haven* explained:

> *Flight quarters! That's all we heard. Day and night. And we all knew what it meant. More wounded from the front.*
>
> *The men in heavy, Mars-like asbestos fire suits stood ready for any tragedy as the control man guided the helicopter to a safe landing. As the noisy motors decreased to a jerky idle and the "All Clear" was given by the pilot, a small band of litter bearers crouched their way to the machine and lifted the patients out carefully, but swiftly.*
>
> *At this point the medical officer made his initial inspection, determining the needs of the patient. If the patient was in a critical condition, plasma and oxygen were available in the well-stocked emergency locker adjacent to the flight deck.*
>
> *Those patients not critically injured were sent to a screening point within the hospital for distribution to the various wards. Time was the vital factor . . . and the movements of men and equipment had to be practically flawless.*
>
> *A voice on the PA system called, "Litter bearers. Man your embarkation stations," and we knew the patients had arrived.*
>
> *The patients continued to stream in, sometimes with great pressure, sometimes just a trickle. The doctors, nurses and corpsmen never stopped administering comfort and treatment to the less fortunate. There was always something to do.*

This Korean cruise was much the same story as the two previous ones, 3,325 patients were admitted and treated. The *Haven* brought back the first repatriated American prisoners of war freed by the Communists in "Operation Rainbow."

Sgt. Harry Clinton Smart, USMC (Ret), recalls a very special nurse aboard the *Haven*:

> *We had just come off the line and were in reserve. The armistice was only a few short months away and the North Koreans were trying desperately to retake as much real estate as possible. The North Koreans had begun a major offensive on 25 March 1953 against the Nevada*

Cities outposts (Reno, Vegas and Carson). We were called out of reserve to reinforce the marines on Vegas.

At approximately 0230 hours on 29 March 1953, my right lower chest and right hip were critically wounded by incoming mortar rounds on OP Vegas.

My journey home began with litter bearers taking me off Vegas hill. My first stop was an aid station (MASH) where they prepared me for the helicopter flight to the hospital ship, Haven. I slipped in and out of consciousness.

I am not sure when I landed on the Haven. I regained consciousness on or about 3 or 4 April 1953. We sailed for Japan several days later landing at Naval Hospital Yokosuka.

Had it not been for the dedicated doctors and nurses who labored nearly ten hours to mend my wounds, I wouldn't be writing today. All the corpsmen, nurses and doctors did an outstanding job.

Although I became acquainted with many nurses and corpsman, there is one, who even today, forty-three years later, still stands out. Her name was Crosby. I don't know her first name or rank. We nicknamed her Bing.

She was never too busy to spend some extra time with those of us who were in very bad shape. She would stop and listen to some guy who really needed attention. Sometimes she took someone's hand and just held it for a few minutes, or she put her arm around someone who had to cope with the loss of a limb, or in some cases multiple limbs.

One day, while doing her job, she stopped in the midst of several bunks and took my hand. While tears ran down her face, she said to all of us patients around her, "I don't know how you boys do what you do in combat. I will never forget you." And I have never forgotten her. [68]

Nurse "Bing" is Comdr. Nancy J. Crosby, Nurse Corps, U.S. Navy (Ret). She says:

I grew up in a big house, three stories and a basement, in Baltimore, Maryland. We had boarders in two rooms to help pay the expenses and one of our boarders was a nurse. I think she influenced my decision to become a nurse. I remember I liked to "fix things." I wanted to fix people, get them well. I graduated from the Union Memorial Hospital nurses' program in 1947.

Both of my brothers were in the navy. My older brother graduated from the Naval Academy and my younger brother enlisted and served aboard submarines. But I was the only one who had to go to war.

During the Korean War I worked mostly in the surgical wards. I served aboard the Haven from 1952-1953. We had eighteen-hour days when the fighting was intense, but the soldiers were working much harder.

During the Korean War, I had a great deal of job satisfaction, but I cried at the thought of some of the injuries . . . those guys were so young.

In January 2000, almost fifty years later, Harry C. Smart, USMC (Ret), was finally able to write his nurse "Bing" to thank her.

The camaraderie aboard the hospital ships was not prevalent just among U.S. medical staff and patients, but extended to the international team, the United Nations soldiers who also were onboard as patients. Language and culture may have been obstacles to precise communication but caring and giving was universal. The spirit of humanity spans all nationalities as an international language.

Gy. Sgt. Donald Mahoney, USMC (Ret), recalls his experience with Greek and Turkish soldiers:

On 17 June 1951 in Central Korea, I was hit with shrapnel in my left leg above the knee while on temporary duty with Machine Gun Section (D Company, Second Battalion, Seventh Marines FMF).

Shortly after I was injured, I was taken to the Haven, anchored in Pusan, Korea. The night after surgery I was having a rough time. I kept recalling how my marine buddies got killed and wounded right next to me. I remember the nurse and the corpsman staying with me all night, trying to comfort me.

I was a corporal and had just turned twenty. The next day two soldiers, a Greek and a Turk, both about twenty-five-years old, came and put me in a wheel chair. Together they wheeled me all round the ship. They didn't speak English, but I guess they took a liking to me. They pushed me around in my wheel chair day and night. Sometimes, they'd even come and wake me at night and motion "come-on" to me.

One night the nurse asked that we sleep at night and said they could push me around during the day. I guess the nurses felt sorry for us and bent some of the rules and let us do our thing.

The Turks made good patients. They were tough, never complaining and didn't want anesthesia for minor operations. Crosby recalls their antics:

I remember the Turkish patients. If we got too close to them, we'd get pinched, but it was hard to avoid since the bunks were so close together.

The *Haven* received nine battle stars for her Korean War service. On 4 January 1954, she departed Long Beach for her fourth Korean cruise. The hostilities were over, but there still were sick and wounded military and civilians.

Do what you can, with what you have, where you are.

Theodore Roosevelt

9

Ambassadors of Goodwill

Whether they were anchored in Pusan, Inchon, Hungnam, or anywhere in Korean waters, the big white ships with the bright red crosses became known as sanctuaries. The wounded, the critically injured, the sick, and the battle fatigued knew they could find solace aboard the hospital ships *Consolation, Repose,* and *Haven.* In addition to caring for U.S. and UN soldiers, frequently the ships' medical crews cared for Korean civilians who had been caught in the crossfire of war.

Captain Brooks recalls that the United Nations troops who were treated aboard the *Consolation* comprised eleven nationalities:

We had patients from all services and all nationalities. There was a tremendous number of different languages and diets. It wasn't easy. They tried to have interpreters for each nationality.

We had Colombians, Turks, Spaniards, Frenchmen, and Italians. The British, Scots, and Australians were easy. It was always very hard for the Turks. When we went from patient to patient, I can remember vividly how we'd have to go from one language to another. Sometimes we'd have to go through four languages before we could speak to the patient.

We could see the terror in their eyes. They didn't understand what was going to happen to them. Of course a lot of them weren't conscious enough to hear anything. But when they were alert enough, we tried to explain what we were trying to do [and] what was going to be done to them. It was very difficult.

I remembered one case. I think we had an Italian who spoke French and a Frenchman [who] spoke Greek. I think the Greek could speak Turkish. That's how complicated it got.

HM1 Smith remembers the Turkish patients:

> I was trying to help a Turkish patient. One of the corpsmen wanted to stick his finger for a blood specimen. The corpsman holding the lancet was nervous. The Turk was a huge guy. We were trying to explain that [we were] going to stick just his finger and we were apologizing, so he grabbed the needle from the corpsman and jabbed his hand.
>
> He said, "I'm a Turk!" We stood there for a moment and then we all laughed. He laughed. We then went on with the treatment and it went well.

International patients made an impression on Lieutenant Commander Kittilson onboard the *Repose:*

> I remember the Turks. The doctor said the Turks all had belly wounds. This meant they charged ahead. They never turned their back on the enemy. We had Ethiopians. I remember them because they were always barefoot. I don't know how they could be barefoot in cold weather.

Lieutenant Commander Kittilson remembers an Englishman:

> I remember an English boy. I think he broke an arm. When he was ready to leave, he put on his kilts. And of course I didn't know much about kilts. He asked me if I would tie his shoes. He was a real character.
>
> He put his foot up on a chair. I had to bend down to tie his shoes. All the patients swarmed around us. Everyone was watching intently. I didn't know at the time what they were up to. Afterward, they asked me, "Does he wear underwear under the kilts?" I couldn't say; I didn't look.

Communicating with someone who does not speak the same language is difficult. It's even more of a challenge when dealing with medical concerns. M. Gy. Sgt. Kurt Loewy, USMC (Ret), was assigned to Fifth Marine and Seventh Marines as a combat photographer:

> I was wounded while with the Seventh Marines on Hill 673 in an area called the Punchbowl and evacuated to the Repose.
>
> In my little corner of the ward we had a wounded French soldier who was unable to speak English. Two volunteer nurses from another ward could communicate with him and that saved the day.

We heard a rumor that the French soldier was to be transferred to a facility where he could communicate with medical personnel, but because the nurse could speak with him, we were able to keep our "French soldier."

In January 1951, the *Jutlandia,* a Danish hospital ship, docked at Pusan, arriving several weeks after the *Repose* and remaining for most of the year.

Photo courtesy of Navy Bureau of Medicine and Surgery Archives (BUMED)
Swedish and Danish nurses have lunch in the wardroom of the *Repose* off the coast of Korea. (left to right) Lt. Roberta A. Ohrman, chief nurse, *Repose;* Sister Ester Sevenson of Stockholm; Lt. Eveline Kittilson, *Repose;* 2d Lt. Faleaciaus of Copenhagen.

The nurses were invited to other UN ships in port. Commander Haire, on the *Consolation,* recalls going aboard a British ship:

7 May 1951. Tonight we had happy hour. The crew from the British cruiser, Kenya, put on a show.

And sometimes the *Consolation,* a highly visible stalwart ship, stopped to help the little guy in trouble. Lieutenant Commander Mangold describes an incident with a small Korean boat:

We were in very choppy waters and someone spotted a little Korean boat loaded with refugees and having a rough time. It was really awful. So we tied her on to the back of the Consolation. As far as I know, we took them to safety somewhere.

Photo courtesy of Helen Brooks
Consolation rescues a small Korean boat and pulls it out of harm's way.

Korean Orphans

In the wake of war's devastation, the innocent and most vulnerable became victims, and so it was that many Korean children were left orphans. In response, navy nurses of the *Consolation* spent many off duty hours caring for sick and injured children, giving physicals and inoculations.

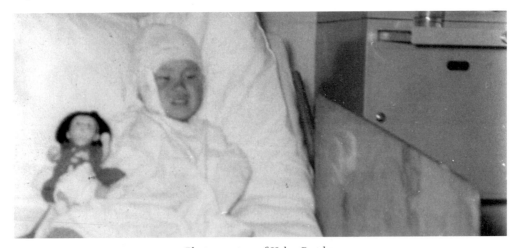

Photo courtesy of Helen Brooks
Young patient with head injury aboard the *Consolation.*

Some of the children came from POW camps outside of Pusan. Some already were in orphanages. A policewoman in Inchon ran one orphanage and Sister Philomena and the Sisters of Charity of St. Vincent de Paul ran the other, St. Paul's orphanage. The *Repose* "adopted" the Happy Mountain Orphanage in Pusan.

Photo courtesy of Helen Brooks
Louise, Mary Jane, Helen Brooks with North Korean children in a POW camp.

Commander Haire wrote about the Korean orphans at St. Paul's Orphanage:

> *6 April 1952. Inchon is considerably cleaner than Pusan and much of the rubble has been cleared away. We went to the large Catholic church, St. Paul's, encountered the orphans and never did get away from them. They were starved for affection and entranced with my nail polish and silk stockings. Poverty was evident but the place was clean. There was one American nun and the rest were Korean.*

Photo courtesy of Helen Brooks
Sister Philomena of St Paul's Orphanage with a young orphan. Navy nurses spent many off duty hours giving physicals, inoculations, and caring for sick children at St Paul's.

The orphans made an impact on Lieutenant Commander Dalton (*Consolation*):

The orphans thought it was great to rub against our stockings, their hands running up and down, up and down our legs. But they were wonderful kids.

And of course we went over there and treated them.

The orphans sat on the beds with their legs underneath them. . . . Of course they didn't understand English too well, so they were a little difficult to take care of.

But after awhile they realized what we wanted. They knew they were being taken care of. They were very interesting. Sometimes we had the Korean children on board the hospital ship.

Photo courtesy of Helen Brooks

Children from an orphanage run by a policewoman in Inchon come aboard the *Consolation* to say thank you. They are singing "The Happy Farmer."

The marines were so good to them. We sent one little Korean youngster down to the dentist. Somehow he had found out about the tooth fairy, and of course he had to have the tooth fairy put something under his pillow, you know. So one of the marines made sure that he was visited by the tooth fairy.

Commander Haire wrote about the Korean orphans in her journal:

29 January 1952. Pusan. We had a belated Christmas party for thirty orphans, fifteen girls and fifteen boys. First we took them into the showers, then dried them, and dressed them in their new clothes. They looked adorable. The patients and crew fought to adopt them for the afternoon.

In the mess hall the children entertained us first by dancing and singing then [they] . . . were given toys and lunch.

Photo courtesy of Marion Haire
Children celebrate the New Year.

The *Repose* assisted the Korean orphanages also when in port. To celebrate the one-year anniversary of the *Repose* in Pusan, the ship had a party for the orphans at the Happy Mountain Orphanage in Pusan. There were about 500 children assembled for the party. They purchased bolts of flannel to make clothes, and purchased books, toys, games, and candy. Through an interpreter, the commanding officer explained that the big white ship was having a party to celebrate being in Pusan for a year.

While in Inchon, the nurses as well as other ships' company visited the Star of the Sea Orphanage. The *Repose* had a party for this orphanage also.

On 20 September 1952, ship's company and medical personnel went ashore with ample supplies of ice cream, cookies and candy. A "Hill-Billy"

Photo courtesy of Helen Brooks
Children asking for chewing gum and candy.

orchestra from the Repose provided musical entertainment . . . refreshments [followed].

A substantial sum of money was given to the Catholic sisters to help defray expenses of providing food and clothing and other necessities for the children. It was a very picturesque setting in war-torn Inchon . . . American sailors in white, entertaining the little children, serving them ice cream, cake and candy.

Morale and Goodwill

Ice cream was a real morale booster in the Korean theater of operations. Whenever the *Repose* was at Inchon, Chinnampo, Pohang-Dong and Pusan, the ship received requests from small naval units and shore stations for ice cream.

Ice cream was one of the first foods patients requested when they could eat solid food and ambulatory patients took care of their friends in the wards. There were times when the ship could not keep up with the demand for ice cream. The ship had 549 officers and men and usually a heavy load of patients. The maximum capacity on the ship was 780. This created a lot of requests for ice cream. Several times the soda fountain was closed temporarily because they just could not meet the demand.

Because the ship maintains its own galley, they helped provide hot meals to other units. When the *Repose* was in Chinnampo in November 1950, the army requested assistance in preparing Thanksgiving dinner. The army provided all the ingredients and the navy crew aboard the *Repose* prepared Thanksgiving dinner. They served over 700 army personnel as well as the entire ship's company, which was close to 700 patients and personnel.

Christmas

With patients coming aboard from the Chosin Reservoir, Christmas 1950 was not a traditional one. Captain Brooks remembers:

The corpsmen did a great job decorating the ship. They were certainly imaginative . . . given the few resources they had. I remember the Christmas tree outside of the OR that kept falling down. The trunk was made of a swab handle. Branches were coat hangers with strips of green dyed sterile wrapping paper. They filled light bulbs with colored water. Cotton balls were strung like popcorn. Icicles were fringed foil wrap. And the poor little tree outside the OR kept falling down.

Photo courtesy of Helen Brooks
The makeshift Christmas tree that corpsmen made kept falling down outside of the OR.

Lieutenant Commander Mangold retells what they did on Christmas Eve *1950*:

*We were right off the beach when they took Hungnam. The ship was to-
tally filled with patients. We didn't have another inch of space on that
ship. We were slowly pulling away from the pier, getting underway,
bound for Yokosuka.*

*The battleship Missouri was shooting over our bow. As the marines
say, "they were softening the beach." They were bombing the beach so we
could pull out of there. Our skipper took us out about midnight. We could
have been shot out of the water so easily. That was Christmas 1950.*

*It was just a little scary. We thought it was New Year's Eve. We could
see all the firing. I remember that so vividly.*

Christmas 1951 aboard the *Consolation* was much more traditional. The ship
even celebrated Christmas Mass. HM1 Smith remembers:

*There was a corpsman named Lake, a third class petty officer, a reservist
and a little older than the average third class. He was a choir director*

Photo courtesy of Helen Brooks
HM3 Lake led the choir and made those who could not carry a tune sound great.

*back home. Boy, he really was a help to us. He formed choirs. He had
people singing that couldn't carry a note in a bucket. But with Lake, they
sounded good.*

Humor

During intense times, a sense of humor can do a world of good. HM1 Smith remembers Navy Nurse McBride:

*Nurse McBride. I think her first name was Birdie. Birdie McBride. Or
at least that's what they called her. She was a great nurse. I think she
was an older gal. She was a senior lieutenant and the ward supervisor.
She had a great sense of humor. A very talented lady.*

    *We'd be as busy as we could be in the ward. She'd want to know if
everybody had their orange juice yet. She'd come bustling by like a little
Gray Lady. We'd laugh so hard. And she'd be climbing up and down
those bunks in her nurse uniform. We'd see her climbing up a bunk.
Everyone would say, "Gee, that's Birdie McBride. I can recognize her
from any angle." She wanted to make sure the guys were comfortable.
She was a good lady.*

Lieutenant Commander Mangold remembers how the corpsmen used humor
to ease the tension:

*Our wards had bunk beds. There were only two orthopedic beds that
were welded to the deck. These beds had all the traction gear and over-*

head bars and trapeze bars and weights. That was where we put the pa-
tients who had the worst injuries. I had wonderful corpsmen. Some of
them were reserves who were called back for the Korean War. One of my
very favorites was a corpsman named Lake, a mortician in civilian life,
and he had a beautiful singing voice. He sang for the church services.

One day we had a patient who was seriously injured. A corpsman and I
were putting him in traction. He was in so much pain and we were trying
hard not to cause him any more. The entire ward was quiet. Everyone was
feeling for this guy. It was tense. Lake came into the ward and watched us
and shook his head. "You always hear of guys with their butts in a sling.
This is the first time I've ever seen a guy with his butt in a sling."

Of course everybody in the ward fell apart. Everyone was laughing so
hard, even the patient.

We had three nurses on the ship who were World War II Veterans.
They were older gals with gray hair. They had really seen their share of
wounded. When Lake saw these nurses in the ward, he would turn to the
guys whose eyes were bandaged. He'd say, "Oh my goodness, you ought to
see this one. She is a knock out. She would make Lana Turner look holy."

The *Consolation* was one of the first hospital ships to have a female doctor.
HM1 Smith remembers her as being impressive:

I think her last name was Walters. Her first name might have been
something like Burma. She was a very prominent surgeon. She was very
good. She was a typical surgeon . . . do things right or you were going to
hear about it. She made one of the popular magazines, either Time or
Life. They had a story about her.

Photo courtesy of Helen Brooks
Burma Walter, M.D., was the first female doctor aboard the USS *Consolation*.

Camaraderie

There was a lot of camaraderie aboard the *Consolation*. Lieutenant Commander Mangold describes it:

> *When you live and work together. You can't help but get close. There were always people who were clowns, people who enjoyed cutting up and having fun.*
>
> *We used to do a lot of singing. I played the piano in the wardroom and the organ for the church services. We always had a lot of fun. Our fun was always very innocent.*
>
> *I wore the nose and glasses when we had birthday parties each month. We celebrated everybody's birthday.*
>
> *We had two wardrooms: one for the doctors and the ship's officers and the other for the nurses. We couldn't eat with the doctors, but for birthdays they'd come to ours, and vice versa.*

Lieutenant Commander Dalton remembers Lieutenant Commander Mangold with the comic nose:

> *Floy Mangold would put on a false nose and big glasses. Then she'd take an old suitcase, pile things in it, and then come running out saying, "I'm going. I've got to get out of here." She'd run toward the deck and everything would fly out of her suitcase. She'd have us all laughing. She was really funny.*

Photo courtesy of Helen Brooks
When times were stressful aboard the *Consolation*, navy nurse Floy Mangold would wear her "nose"
and entertain the troops.

Lieutenant Commander Dalton added that the marines were also part of the team:

> *Most of the time you didn't have to ask the marines to help, and if you'd ask them, they would do it. They would feed patients. They help with the patients. When the new patients came in, they would cut their clothes off. This helped us see where the patient was wounded.*
>
> *We had patients who were completely burned. They had to have a lot of fluid. The marines would make sure they got what they needed. You would never have to ask a marine to help another marine.*

Parties provided a means of relaxation and a way to change focus for a few hours. By the end of October, the patient load was stabilized. So, the *Consolation* had a Halloween party. Commander Haire remembered some of the costumes:

> *Three of the men came as Korean men in stove pipe hats, white robes and goatees. The exec [executive officer] came in evening dress, complete except for trousers.*
>
> *I almost forgot the Jack-o-Lanterns. The doctors used . . . volley balls, put a plaster cast around them . . . colored them orange.*

Photo courtesy of Helen Brooks
Joe Witt, Sammy Weiss, Gale Clark and Blyne Gumm got dressed up as Korean gentlemen
for the Halloween party.

Motivated by patriotism, and a strong desire to maximize their nursing skills, navy nurses of the Korean War performed beyond expectations. No one can maintain this stress and work level indefinitely, but nursing and other medical staff knew how to take care of themselves, to endure a long siege and then to rejuvenate in mind and spirit. When patient loads tapered off, nurses went to movies or parties to escape and focus on some fun. Then they could return to their high-paced environment, refreshed, and energized.

Photo courtesy of Helen Brooks
(Left to right) Rodney May, Royal Navy, with Helen Brooks and Dr. Erec, NMS *Kenya* (British cruiser).

Photo courtesy of Helen Brooks
(Left to right) Lieutenants Haire and Brooks with two Korean generals.

Photo courtesy of Eveline Kittilson McClean

Pusan: Lieutenant Kittilson with two Korean navy nurses, a Danish nurse and Eileen Ferrel from the *Repose*.

Photo courtesy of Marion Haire

Inchon: May 1952. Lieutenant Haire with two young patients, "Joe" (left) and "Mike."

Epilogue

Forgotten No More

It has been fifty years since 3,000 navy nurses made an unselfish commitment to our nation to serve during the Korean War. These quiet heroes, undaunted by adversity, cared for their patients from breadth of their skills and the depths of their hearts and souls.

After the Korean War, some continued their navy careers. Other chose to become nursing professionals in the civilian sector. Many married and raised families.

Fifty years later the navy nurses of the Korean War, now in their 70s, 80s, and 90s, still exude the undaunted faith that "it will all work out," and the resilience to bounce back from adversity, allowing themselves to re-juggle their plans and go down a different route. Their contagious, effervescent spirit still fills rooms wherever they are.

> *God bless you and thanks for being so patient with us until we could be free once again. Thanks for looking our way as you sped to work past our lonely bunks. Semper Fidelis to the navy nurses! I was the first grad from the amputee center in Oakland, California, from the Korean War.*
>
> **Pfc Herbert Luster, USMC (Ret)**

> *I thank [them]. . . . My deepest respect to the U.S. Navy Nurses Corps of the Korean War. God Bless and keep them in the palm of his hand.*
>
> **S. Sgt. William B. Chain, Jr., USMC (Ret)**

> *I would apologize to them for the tremendous physical and emotional burden they endured for us, the wounded. I never saw one of them flinch in the face of the flood of broken and helpless marines that was brought to them from the Korean battlefields. In September 1951, I was one of the wounded. The nurses and corpsmen made every effort to put us back*

*together again the way we were before injury . . . Neither government
nor individual can ever compensate them for what they gave. In the next
life God will treat them as special as they deserve, one and all.*

S. Sgt. Michael Maurphy, USMC (Ret)

Photo courtesy of Tommy Smith

Korea, 1951: Tommy E. Smith, USMC, was a machine gunner.
"I planned to make a career and stay for thirty years."

Photo courtesy of Tommy Smith

Nurses who Tommy Smith came in contact with during the Korean War changed his life.
"Nurses converted me [into] a loving and caring person, and I wanted to be just like them,
relieving pain. After my honorable discharge . . . I was the first full-time male student to graduate
from . . . nursing school. Five years later I was a Certified Registered Nurse Anesthetist."
Tommy Smith has been a nurse for forty-three years.

Photo courtesy of Carola Braun Gradilone
Yokosuka nurse Carola Braun Gandilone visiting San Diego.

Photo courtesy of Frances Omori
(Left to right) Jean Ellis Young, Marilyn Ewing Affleck, Joan Heath Steyn and Lura Jane Emery.

Photo courtesy of Lois Merritt
Lois Merritt.

Photo courtesy of Helen Fable
Helen Fable and Tiger.

Photo courtesy of Helen Brooks
Helen Brooks celebrating her eightieth birthday in 1999.

Photo courtesy of Lois Merritt
(Left to right) Katie Shields Randall, Lois Merritt, Nell Chumley Long (deceased), Vila Knuth Allen
and Lillian Wojnarowski Golden.

Photo courtesy of Lura Jane Emery
(Left to right) Lillian Orihel (deceased), Eveline Kittilson McClean, Lura Jane Emery.

Photo courtesy of Betty J. Alexander
Betty Jo Alexander, known to her friends as B.J. or Alex.

Photo courtesy of James Robert Standing

Young corpsman Standing stationed at Camp Pendleton with Marilyn Ewing and Betty J. Alexander. He later served aboard the *Consolation* and saw Ewing and Alexander when the ship put into port in Yokosuka.

Photo courtesy of Marilyn Ewing Affleck

(Left to right) Pat Standing, James Robert Standing and Marilyn Ewing Affleck.

Photo courtesy of Harry Sorenson
Hazel Sorenson served aboard the *Haven* during the Korean War.

For fifty years many have wanted to say thank you, and for fifty years they have been frustrated because they could not say thank you. Most cannot say thank you enough.

Navy nurses of the Korean War,
the quiet heroes,
are forgotten no more.

Appendix 1

Recruiting Poster for Military Nurses

JOIN
The Army or Navy as Nurses

FROM Iceland to New Guinea—from India to North Africa—wherever our armed forces are stationed —on land or on sea or in the air--thousands of American nurses are serving in this global war.

Uniformed in smart khaki or blue, as officers in the Army and Navy Nurse Corps, these gallant women are doing the indispensable job of giving nursing care to their brothers in uniform who are in training or fighting at home and abroad.

Thousands more are NEEDED. Will YOU come in? Choose your service and sign up today at your nearest Red Cross chapter.

The American National Red Cross
Washington, D. C.

Courtesy of Carola Braun Gradilone

Appendix 2
Navy Nurse Requirements

To become a Navy nurse. and a commissioned officer in the United States Navy. a nurse must be:

★ An American citizen
★ Unmarried
★ Between 21 and 29 years old
★ A registered nurse of nursing
★ Graduate of a recognized school
★ Able to meet physical. mental and moral standards for naval officers.

Complete information on how to join the Navy Nurse Corps. and application forms. may be obtained at any Office of Naval Officer Procurement. These are located in the 17 cities listed below. If none of these is convenient to your home. write to the Navy Nurse Corps. Bureau of Medicine and Surgery, Navy Department. Washington 25, D. C.

BOSTON, ... New Court & PO Bldg.	MACON. . . . . . . Post Office Bldg.
CHICAGO. . . . . 844 N. Rush Street	MINNEAPOLIS. . N. Western Bank Bldg.
CINCINNATI, ... Court & PO Bldg.	NEW ORLEANS. . . . . Bienville Hotel
DALLAS. . . . . Terminal Annex Bldg.	NEW YORK. . . . . . . 346 Broadway
DENVER. . . . New U. S. Customs House	PHILADELPHIA. . . . 13 S. 13th Street
DETROIT. . . . . . New Federal Bldg.	PITTSBURGH. . . . . Old Federal Bldg.
KANSAS CITY. . . . . U. S. Courthouse	SAN FRANCISCO. . . . . Federal Bldg.
LOS ANGELES. . . . 626 S. Spring St.	SEATTLE. . . . . Federal Office Bldg.
WASHINGTON. D. C.. 1400 Penn. Ave. N. W.	

Appendix 3

Meritorious Unit Commendation

The Secretary of the Navy takes pleasure in commending

UNITED STATES NAVAL HOSPITAL
YOKOSUKA, JAPAN

for service as follows:

"For extremely meritorious service in the treatment
and hospitalization of 5804 war casualties and other patients from
5 December 1950, to 15 January 1951. Although still in the process of expanding from a 100-bed dispensary to an 800-bed hospital,
the United States Naval Hospital, Yokosuka, Japan, admitted and
treated 4312 casualties during the 10-day period from 5 to 15
December, 2022 of whom were received during the peak period
of 6-7 December 1950. Interested solely in saving lives and
bringing physical comfort to the increasing stream of wounded;
the staff exerted maximum effort in preparing additional space
for the proper care of its patients. With the already inadequate
facilities tremendously overtaxed, the limited number of personnel
worked long, arduous hours, sacrificing much-needed rest to provide medical treatment and other essential services to this overwhelming patient overload caused almost wholly by the influx of
United States Marine Corps members who had been wounded when
suddenly trapped by aggressor forces in the Choshin Reservoir
area. By its resourcefulness, zeal and initiative in the face of
many complex adversities, this gallant organization saved the lives
of numerous casualties, thereby upholding the highest traditions
of the United States Naval Service."

All personnel attached to and serving with the United States Naval Hospital,
Yokosuka, Japan, from 5 December 1950, to 15 January 1951, are hereby
authorized to wear the NAVY UNIT COMMENDATION Ribbon.

Secretary of the Navy

Appendix 4
Naval Hospital Yokosuka Christmas Menu

CHRISTMAS GREETINGS

UNITED STATES NAVAL HOSPITAL
YOKOSUKA, JAPAN
25 DECEMBER 1950

Courtesy of John Cook

CHRISTMAS MENU

FRUIT

COCKTAIL CUP

CELERY STICKS   SWEET PICKLES

RIPE-GREEN OLIVES   CRANBERRY SAUCE

ROAST YOUNG TURKEY

GIBLET GRAVY   WHIPPED WHITE POTATOES

CHESTNUT DRESSING

FRESH FROZEN BUTTERED CAULIFLOWER

FRESH FROZEN GREEN PEAS

MAYONNAISE DRESSING   TOSSED GREEN SALAD

FRENCH DRESSING

PUMPKIN PIE WITH WHIPPED CREAM   ICE CREAM

FRUIT CAKE

DINNER   ROLLS   BUTTER   COFFEE   MILK

CIGARS

CIGARETTES

MIXED NUTS

HARD CANDIES

CHRISTMAS MESSAGE

As another Christmas dawns, the weather of the visible world is threatening—problems fester, issues become clouded with the darkness of men's errors. The bonds of brotherhood are strained by the pull of clamor and the thrust of strife.

But deep in the christian heart there is a brighter climate. Hope springs eternal from the everlasting Christ born on Christmas Day; the light which no darkness can put out. Brotherhood is indestructively woven into the fabric of Christmas.

It is our sincere wish that you and your loved ones will experience a blessed Christmas and the New Year will bring success and happiness as well as a lasting Peace to all mankind.

CAPTAIN W. F. JAMES, MC, USN

COMMANDING OFFICER

CAPTAIN F. J. WEDDELL, JR., MC., USN

EXECUTIVE OFFICER

CHIEF WARRANT OFFICER W. H. BASSETT

HC, USN

CHIEF, COMMISSARY DIVISION

LIEUTENANT M. O'NEILL, NC., USN

DIETITIAN

OFFICER PERSONNEL

MEDICAL CORPS

CAPT W. F. JAMES
CAPT F. J. WEDDELL, JR.
CDR I. E. POTTER
CDR L. F. FRIEND
CDR R. J. WHIPPLE
CDR R. H. WARD
CDR W. H. GULLEDGE
CDR O. T. MC DONOUGH
CDR B. M. SHEPARD
CDR J. D. KING
CDR J. W. METCALFE
LCDR A. E. WENTZ
LCDR G. G. CLARK
LCDR W. W. ROBLEY
LCDR W. B. NEAL, JR.
LCDR H. G. BILLMAN
LT E. R. WOODWARD
LT C. W. DOCKHAM
LT B. A. BELEW
LT J. F. CRAVEN
LT R. E. BOUGHTON
LT A. J. FARRELL, JR.
LT T. E. BANKS, JR.
LTJG N. P. MORIN
LTJG L. W. CONDIE
LTJG D. M. BUTLER
LTJG R. J. KLEINHENZ
LTJG S. D. LUSTERMANN
LTJG S. V. LANDREITH
LTJG W. E. MAYER
LTJG A. D. WATSON
LTJG H. E. WOOD, JR.
LTJG J. H. YOUNG
LTJG D.B. CARMICHAEL, JR.
LTJG T. J. M. BURNETT

LTJG W. R. SILLERY
LTJG P. W. BRAUNSTEIN
LTJG E. F. BUTLER
LTJG T. N. KIRKLAND, JR.
LTJG E. R. MC GOVERN
LTJG G. L. WILSON
LTJG A. V. HOLMES
LTJG O. M. GRAVES, JR.
LTJG F. J. MOORE
LTJG A. L. OVREGAARD
LTJG J. T. PARENTE
LTJG W. R. DANIEL,
LTJG I.E. BECKHAM, JR.
LTJG H. L. HOFFMAN
LTJG M. J. ALEXANDER
LTJG R. B. SARVER
LTJG J. L. KEATING
LTJG J. E. KICKLIGHTER
LTJG J. S. MAUGHON
LTJG H. B. HASTON
LTJG L. B. MERMAN
LTJG J. J. GREENIER
LTJG A. E. BOTWIN
LTJG E. G. LAFORET
LTJG J. PEACOCK
LTJG P. W. SCHNEIDER
LTJG A. G. SHARF
LTJG M. E. SILVERSTEIN
LTJG W. R. THOMAS
LTJG C. WOODS
LTJG V. J. MERKLE
LTJG J. M. POYNTER
LTJG J. H. HARRIS
LTJG R. H. LARSON
CDR J. A. ADDISON

LTJG R. P. DOBBIE, JR.
LTJG D. L. STEPHENS
CDR. C. L. REYNOLDS
LTJG S. B. GUNDERSEN
LTJG S. M. PARISER
LTJG N. F. STONE
LTJG J. J. MC LEOD
LTJG L. J. LAWSON
LTJG J. T. TEASLEY
LTJG M. W. OLSON
LTJG S. R. ORR
CDR R. T. A. KNUDSEN
LTJG F. C. STUBENORD
LTJG D. B. HELLER
LTJG A. E. BOTWIN
LTJG C. W. GAULKINS, JR
LTJG W. G. YOUNG, JR.

LTJG D. D. GADD
LTJG D. T. BROWN
LTJG R. B. LITTLE
LTJG J. BUETTNER
LT R. H. BROWN
CDR A. TROMBETTA
LTJG H. R. BRIDGE
LTJG W. P. JENSEN
LTJG C. M. MC CLURE
LTJG M. E. MUSGRAVE
LTJG R. W. HAYTEN
LTJG W. R. STRONG
LTJG C. E. HORTON
LTJG J. PEACOCK
LT T. E. BANKS, JR.
CDR J. W.METCALF
CDR J. B. ROWE

MEDICAL SERVICE CORPS

LCDR O. L. YOUNG
LCDR O. L. ETHERIDGE
LT C. R. HARVEY
LT W. F. LESTER
LT C. P. CALHOUN
LTJG N. B. CURTIS
LTJG I. E. BYERS
LTJG R. W. EASTMAN

LTJG R. C. RAYBOURN
LTJG M. H. LAMB
LTJG R. L. CANNON
LTJG L. H. JOSLIN
LTJG S. LEWKOWICZ
ENS T. W. DRUMMOND
ENS W. J. MORGAN

HOSPITAL CORPS

CWOHC C. M. NAGLE
CWOHC H. C. WILLIAMS

CWOHC R. O. LOGSDON
CWOHC W. H. BASSETT

CHAPLAIN CORPS

LCDR C. H. SHACKELFORD
LCDR C. W. LAWLOR

LTJG J. E. ZOLLER

LTJG D. L. REDIG
LTJG R. ANDREWS
LTJG R. M. WILLSEY
LTJG M. M. THORNTON
LTJG E. C. CARVILLE
LTJG R. M. ANDERSON
LTJG J. E. ELLIS
LTJG M. F. DALTON
LTJG V. M. RANKIN
LTJG G. BARKER
LTJG M. A. SMITH
LTJG S. A. DOBB
LTJG M. MC CARTHY
LTJG H. M. WEBER
LTJG A. E. ARNEY
LTJG S. Z. BORCHARDT
LTJG H. J. DEMARIANO
LTJG M. S. DODGE
LTJG C. L. READINGER
LTJG M. L. REGAN
LTJG M. D. SHANKS
LTJG M. F. WERSACKAS
LTJG K. L. THOMPSON
LTJG V. M. BALFE
LTJG M. E. GREEN
LTJG D. M. LACONE
LTJG E. E. KOEILER
LTJG R. E. MEARS
LTJG M. C. PRYOR
LTJG M. I. STINE
LTJG E. M. HANKS
LTJG G. A. HART
LTJG R. HAYES
LTJG E. M. MARTIN
LTJG O. R. MURPHY

LT C. H. BRAUN
LT E. M. CALDEN
LT V. A. DAVIS
LT G. HAMLIN
LT M. D. MUJAWSKI
LT D. M. MC ALEES
LT R. M. SCANLON
LTJG F. C. THOMAS
LTJG I. R. LA MARRA
LTJG F. O. ROBERTS
LTJG P. T. SINGLEY
LTJG M. E. MAGUIRE
LTJG R. E. KENNEDY
LTJG M. C. CHILCOTT
LTJG G. J. FRINGLE
LTJG A. L. DAVIS
LTJG F. L. HARRIS
LTJG F. A. SALDEN
LTJG E. V. BAKER
LTJG L. R. ANASTASIA
LTJG C. L. WERNER
LTJG A. J. WILKINSON
LTJG H. F. RICKARD
LTJG I. A. FRIZANOSKY
LTJG L. F. AMLONG
LTJG M. V. MENDELSON
LTJG D. A. ADAM
LTJG P. R. UHORCZUK
LTJG S. J. BURRIS
LTJG C. A. ARMSTRONG
LTJG S. A. WHEELER
LTJG R. J. WILLARD
LTJG A. C. MANGUM
LTJG F. A. MAHER
LTJG M. R. CAVEY

CONSTRUCTION CORPS

LT S. HANSEN

NURSE CORPS

LCDR A. BURKE
LT A. C. BALLANTYNE
LT B. B. AHREND
LT M. A. VAUGHN
LT J. E. COLLINS
LT A. E. ALLGEIER
LT M. M. ZWEIR
LT M. A. COMFORT
LT B. L. FRENCH
LT H. M. DANKO
LT E. M. GIESE
LT I. C. PATRICK
LT L. E. STONAGE
LT M. A. AHRENS
LT F. M. GRIFFITH
LT E. R. RAWSON
LT E. M. FERN
LT H. C. KUSENBERG
LT B. W. SMITH
LT V. D. BARTON
LT E. A. MC QUAID
LT E. F. MAC MILLAN
LT E. C. HAYES
LT F. K. BALL
LT M. F. CRONIN
LT M. E. PRICE
LT M. O'NEILL
LT E. A. BLISS
LT G. DEKLE

LT A. C. FOOTO
LT A. W. HARDING
LT E. D. LARSEN
LT C. M. REULAND
LT R. J. SMALL
LT F. E. SQUIRE
LT F. E. ALWYN
LT L. E. FIDLER
LT B. J. FUNK
LT A. E. GUSTAFSON
LT D. M. HENDRICKS
LT T. C. BAKER
LT V. R. ESTES
LT M. E. HANSEN
LT R. I HILL
LT C. M. EBERT
LT W. K. DE JARNETTE
LT A. M. ANDERSON
LT M. T. MC DONALD
LT D. M. MC MANUS
LT L. I. GOWELL
LT M. A. MARTIN
LT M. B. JENKINS
LT V. R. CHIPMAN
LT M. E. MOREHOUSE
LT C. M. PRUNSKUNAS
LT A. SHIGLO
LT V. A. STEIN
LT H. E. FABLE

ENLISTED PERSONNEL

ALEXANDER, Charles B.	HM3
ALEXANDER, Vasil(n)	HM2
ALLEN, William J.	HM1
ALUMBAUGH,GeorgeW.Jr-	HM3
ANDERSON, Robert L.,	HM2
ANTOINETTE, Santos(n),Jr.	HN
ARCHER, James T.	HM2
ARGAUD, Samuel E.	HMC
ARMBRUST, Albert F.	HM3
ARRAMBIDE, Charles (n)	HM3
ASBILL, Robbie J.	HMC
ASMUNDSON, Gisli (n)	HMC
ATYEO, Warren T.	HM3
AUSLEY, James D.	HM2
AYARS, Donald D.	HN
BACH, Richard B.	HM3
BAGWELL, Carlos D. T.	HMC
BAILEY, Donald J.	HN
BAILA, Stephen L.	HM3
BARABY, Albert G.	HM3
BARD, Raymond G.	ME3
BARNETT, Roland L.	HM2
BARNSLEY, Harry L.	EMP3
BARRY, Donald J.	HM1
BASINGER, William A.	IIN
BATTS, Willis R.	HM3
BATZ, Samson (n)	PNTC
BEINDORFF, Richard M.	HM2
BELLAMY, Jimmie O.	HN
BENSON, John W.	HMC
BESEMER, Arthur R.	HM3
BESIO, Carlo P.	HM3
BIMMERLE, Joseph J.	HM2
BISHOP, Vernon J.	HMC
ACK, Cleo B.	IIN
ACKBURN, James E.	HM1

BLANCKAERT, August C.	IIN
BLASKO, Albert J.	HM2
BLYTHE, Carter, A., Jr.	HM3
BOEHM, Clifton A.	HM3
BOGGS, Malcolm P.	HM3
BOHANNON, Willard E.	HN
BOLEN, Robert H.	HN
BORRESEN, Gerald A.	HN
BOUCHER, Albert N.	HN
BRANCH, John "L"	HM2
BRANT, George C.	HM3
BROWN, Billy H.	HM3
BROWN, Virgil V.	HM1
BRYNGEISON, John E.	HM3
BUCKNER, Franklin J.	HN
BUCKINGHAM, Ralph K.	IIMC
BUDA, Florian P.	HN
BUHRE, John L.	IIM2
BUNCE, Keith M.	HM3
BURGESS, Robert L.	HM3
BURNETT, Howard S.	HM2
BUSCEMI, Anthony P.	HN
CALKINS, Bobbie R.	IIM1
CAPPELL, Albert T.	HM2
CARNEY, Robert D.	IIM1
CARR, Robert L., Jr.	IIMC
CARTER, Harold B., Jr.	HM2
CARTER, Jackie "M"	HM3
CARTER, William B.	IIN
CAUTHEN, Campbell,C, Jr.	IIM2
CERNOVSKY, Frank J.	IIN
CHAMBERS, Frank W.	HN
CHAMBERS, Warren C.	IIM1
CHERRY, James C., Jr.	IIMC
CHIRICHELLO, Angelo J.	HM3
CHRISTIANSEN, Ernest M.	HM3

LTJG B. F. PANTLIK
LTJG E. A. PAUL
LTJG A. E. YOHILLINGER
LTJG B. L. DONAHUE
LTJG V. J. HUFFMAN
LTJG F. ACKERMAN
LTJG D. B COHEN
LTJG I. L. DOOIAN
LTJG I. T. GABOS
LTJG T. F. MAXWELL
LTJG V. A. EASTIN
LTJG M. FAUDREE
LTJG V. L. KNUTH
LTJG M. J. STEWART
LTJG M. E. EDWARDS
LTJG E. C. ROMANO
LTJG L. DZIKEWICZ
LTJG M. J. SKENODORE
LTJG M. F. BRINES
LTJG S. A. CASEY
LTJG G. M. LANG
LTJG C. M. MANGOLD
LTJG I. I. MARTIN
LTJG R. E. STEINER
LTJG C. V. GILLIGAN
LTJG H. SEKIN
ENS V. SMITH
ENS I. HATHAWAY
ENS N. J. SMOOGEN
ENS A. V. HOPPLE
ENS W. E. PIZORKA
ENS A. M. ROBERTS
ENS J. T. ERNST
ENS R. A. GERVAIS
ENS V. M. JENNINGS

ENS A. M. De REYES
ENS B. ELLIS
ENS E. C. RIGGS
ENS E. J. OBRIEN
ENS L. A. POWER
ENS M. E. CARMICKIE
ENS A. A. BERGEN
ENS N. M. CHUMLEY
ENS B. GACHIS
ENS H. S. JOHNSTONE
ENS L. C. MARRITT
ENS D. E. MOORE
ENS M. E. KISSENGER
ENS D. N. SWEETMAN
ENS E. L. CARROLL
ENS L. M. FRANK
ENS L. M. JUDY
ENS M. E. H. OBRIEN
ENS J. B. PIECZARKA
ENS D. L. ROWE
ENS M. B. STRIMM
ENS B. J. ALEXANDER
ENS I. D. DUNAHOO
ENS M. EWING
ENS P. S. HEIMBERGER
ENS L. E. MC BRATNEY
ENS L. RODES
ENS G. J. STERLING
ENS C. R. DUPUIS
ENS J. J. FLOOD
ENS M. E. GLAVIN
ENS M. G. BIERMA
ENS M. M. RYAN
ENS C. L. PIERCE

Name	Rate
GILDAY, John W.	RD2
GILDER, Grady (n)	HM2
GILLEY, Leonard C.	HMC
GIPSON, Rex C.	HM2
GIRARDI, Daniel (n)	HN
GLOSSER, Charles L.	HM2
GODCHAUX, Burton P., Jr.	HN
GOFF, Wade H.	HM1
GOLDWIRE, William P.	HN
GORDON, Richard T.	HN
GRAHAM, Charles D.	HM2
GRANT, John C.	HM2
GRANTHAM, Rodney G., Jr.	HM2
GRAY, Alan I.	MM1e2
GREENE, William E.	HM2
GREWELL, Russell (n)	HM3
GRESHAM, Edward O.	HM1
GRIFFIN, Chan A.	HM1
GWILLIAM, Gilbert F., Jr.	HN2
HAGOPIAN, Arthur M.	HMC
HAINSWORTH, Ralph L.	HM3
HAIR, Sammie N.	HN
HALL, Herbert C.	HM3
HAMEL, Jack N.	HM2
HAMILTON, David E.	HM3
HAMILTON, Donald C.	HM3
HANNA, Mark (n)	HM3
HARLAN, Carl R.	HN
HARMON, Richard D.	HN
HARPER, Norman R.	HM2
HARRIS, George S.	HM2
HARRIS, Jimmy (n)	HM1
HARRIS, William H.	HMC
HART, Dewey D.	HN
HART, Nicholas B.	HN
HATCHER, Portis B.	HM3
HAVINGHORST, Carl R.	HM3
HEENEY, John T.	HM3

Name	Rate
HEIT, Samuel J.	HM1
HENSON, George (n)	HM3
HETTINGER, William F., Jr.	HM3
HIGGINS, Darmon C.	HM3
HIGGINS, Jack M.	HM3
HILL, Willard B.	HM1
HOBERT, Duane F.	HM3
HOFMAIER, Leo A.	HMC
HOLMS, William J. C.	CSG3
HOLT, Theodore J.	HM2
HOLTERMANN, Rudolph J.	HM2
HOOD, Winton C.	HMC
HORNE, James M., Jr.	HM2
HORSTMAN, Paul C.	HM1
HUGHES, Davey L.	HM3
HULL, Virgil E.	HMC
HUMPHREYS, Leonard B.	HM3
HUNDLEY, Bennie L.	HM3
HUNDLEY, Harold D.	HN
HUNNEL, Hugh C.	HN
HUNTER, Robert L.	HN
HURFORD, David C.	HN
IANNARELLI, Anthony N.	HMC
IRVINE, Sidney S.	HN
JACKSON, Jack W.	HM3
JAMES, Paul D.	HMC
JARMAN, Elwood B.	HN
JENKINS, Albert D.	HM1
JENKINS, Bobby C.	HN
JESSOP, Frank H.	HMC
JOHN, Leland (n)	HM1
JOHNSON, Floyd M.	CSR1
JOHNSON, Richard H.	HM2
JONES, Charles I.	HM3
JONES, Raymond S.	HM3
JOST, Erich C.	HN
JULIAN, Harvey E.	HM3

Name	Rate
CINI, Arlington G.	HN
CLARK, Billie P.	HM3
CLARK, James C.	HM3
CLARK, Joe C.	HN
CLARKE, Frederick G.	HN
COHEN, Stanley A.	HM3
COMMONS, Howard W.	HMC
COOMBS, James L.	HN
COOPER, Bertram (n)	HM2
COOPER, Willie (n), Jr.	HN
COPELAND, Benjamin (n)	HM3
COSCIA, James B.	HM3
COVINGTON, James R.	HM2
COWIE, Charles (n), Jr.	HM2
COX, William A.	HM3
CRESS, William C.	HMC
CROCKER, Cleveland D.	HN
CROOKHAM, William S.	HM3
CROTTY, John E.	HM3
CURRY, Richard F.	HM3
DAIGLE, Joseph E. N.	HMC
DAVEY, Neil G.	HM3
DAVIS, Donald P.	HM3
DAVIS, Eugene R.	HN
DAVIS, Junius E.	HM1
DEAN, Willard W.	HM1
DEKEHOE, Joseph R.	HMC
DELANEY, James P.	HN
DENHAM, John D.	HN
DIEHL, James I.	HM2
DILLON, Lawrence B.	HMCA
DONCHIN, Maurice (n)	HM2
DOERING, Bobby G.	HM3
DORFNER, Walter F.	HN
DOWNS, Ora S., Jr.	HM2
DUNLAP, Wilson W.	HMC
DURCAN, John J.	HM2
DYER, Kenneth H.	HM3

Name	Rate
DYKINS, Eugene M.	HM2
EDELL, Jack D.	HMC
ECHEMANN, Howard B.	HMC
ECK, Bruce D.	IM1
EMMONS, Harold E.	IIM1
ENNIS, James N.	HM2
ESTES, Gene (n)	HM1
EVERINGHAM, Richard L.	HM2
FAILING, Earl O.	HM3
FELDER, Bennie E.	HM3
FERGUSON, William R.	HM2
FERIA, Jose "B".	HM3
FIELDS, James C.	HM1
FINE, William S.	HM3
FINN, Lawrence M.	IIMC
FINNERAN, Hilary A.	IM1
FITZPATRICK, Thomas J.	IIM2
FLEMING, Carl I.	IM1
FORD, Edward M.	HM3
FORD, William J.	HN
FORBES, William A.	HM2
FOWLER, Frank M.	HM2
FROST, Louis C.	IM1
FRY, Maurice E.	HN
FULLINGTON, Raymond E.	HMC
GALI, Jacob (n)	HM3
GALLAGHER, Matthew W.	HM3
GAMBILL, Vernon M.	HN
GANNARD, Russel J.	HM2
GARCIA, Raymond (n)	HM3
GARRETT, Louis G.	HN
GARRISON, James C.	HM2
GARRISON, Kendall E.	HM3
GAST, James E.	IIM3
GEIGER, Gordon R.	IIA
GERMANY, Theodore P.	HM2
GERRANS, Benjamin L.	HM2

Name	Rank
JURGENSON, Jack L.	HM3
KADDATZ, John K.	HN
KADLEC, Frank J.	HMC
KALEBJIAN, Harry (n)	HN
KAUFMAN, William B.	HN
KELLY, Elborn D.	HM3
KENNALLY, James R.	HMC
KIMMONS, David E., Jr.	HN
KING, Ainslee W. N.	HMC
KING, William F.	HMC
KINGERY, Richard E.	HN
KLEIN, Robert L.	HMC
KLINGLER, John F.	HM1
KOOIMAN, William(n), Jr.	HM3
KOPFER, Rudolph(n), Jr.	EMP1
KUBE, William E.	HN
KUZMA, William F.	HM3
LACKEY, Roscoe G.	HM2
LALLY, Thomas J.	HN
LANDIS, Milton (n)	HN
LANDRY, Arthur J.	HM1
LANGLAIS, Theodore J.	HM1
LA VALLEY, John H.	HM1
LAWSON, Frederick W.	HM2
LENNEY, George B.	HM1
LESTER, Billy B.	HM3
LINDSEY, Wayne A.	HN
LIPPENCOTT, Walter F.	HM1
LONG, Dorrance A.	HMC
LONGANECKER, Walter S.	HN
LONGNECKER, Max W.	HM1
LORENZ, Marvin G.	HM1
LUBER, Arthur H.	HMC
LYONS, Donald A.	HM1
MADDY, Howard R.	HM3
MADSEN, David W.	HMC
MAIER, Edward M.	HM2
MARSHALL, Bernard E.	HM3

Name	Rank
MASSIE, William R.	CSG3
MAXWELL, Clendon L.	HM2
MAXWELL, Billy L.	HM2
MAY, Vernon L.	DCP1
MC CLAIN, Russell A.	HN
MC CLOSKY, John M.	HM3
MC CUAN, Randall H.	HM3
MC LAIN, Kenneth B.	HM3
MC LAINE, William F.	HM2
MC MILLAN, Albert C.	HM1
MC PHERSON, Edward P.	HM3
MEADOWS, Phillip E.	HM3
MEEKS, Boyd E.	HM3
MEREDITH, James R.	HM3
MEREDITH, Carl J., Jr.	HM2
MERNICK, Edward J.	HM3
MIDDLETON, Howard E.	HM2
MILLER, Harold (n)	HM2
MILLER, Ronald P.	HN
MIMS, Franklin C.	HM3
MINK, George W.	HM1
MISKOVICH, James J.	HM3
MONICA, James (n)	HM2
MONROE, Verl "R"	HMC
MOORE, Billy L.	HN
MOORE, Floyd W.	HM1
MOORE, Francis C.	HN
MOORE, William W.	HM3
MORGAN, John(n), Jr.	HM3
MORIN, Frank F.	HM1
MORRIS, James D.	HN
MORRIS, Ralph (n)	HM3
MORRISON, Richard J.	HN
MORROW, James W.	CS3
MORROW, Mahlon G.	HN
MOSS, Arthur W.	HMC
MOTT, "J" "D"	HM2
MYERS, Charles D.	HM3

Name	Rank
NAY, Glen M.	HM2
NEFF, Kenneth S.	HM3
NEIDLINGER, Paul E.	HM2
NEEDHAM, Robert O.	DCC
NELSON, Frank R.	HM1
NICHOLAS, Charles (n)	HMC
NICHOLSON, Earl C.	HN
NIMITS, William (n)	HM2
NORDSTROM, Murl E.	TE3
NORRIS, George E.	HM2
NORTON, John H.	HM1
NOVAK, John D.	HM3
NOYES, Vincent L.	HMC
OAKES, Harry A.	HMC
O'DELL, James F.	HM2
ODLE, Kenneth L.	HN
OGLE, James H.	HN
O'KEEFFE, Jimmy W.	HN
OLDHAM, Ralph L.	HM1
OLIVER, James R.	HMC
PALONE, Robert C.	HM2
PARR, Floyd E.	HM2
PARSONS, Wilbur J.	HN
PATER, John J.	HMC
PAUK, John F.	HM2
PEARSON, William G.	HM3
PEEKS, Thomas E.	HMC
PENZIEN, Carlton B.	HM3
PERRY, Billie J.	SA
PERRY, Lionel R.	FA
PESTANA, Adolph (n)	HM3
PETERSON, Max R.	HMC
PHILLIPS, Clarence H.	HM1
PICKERING, Robert K.	SA
PIERCE, George H.	HM1
PIERCE, George S.	SA
PIERCE, James A.	SA
PITMAN, Kyle "C"	SA
PITTS, Charles I.	SA

Name	Rank
PLATNICK, Allen H.	HM1
PRICE, William B.	HN
PRINGLE, Alwyn T.	HM1
PRISCO, Pasquale V.	HN
RAE, Donald W.	HM1
RANDOLPH, Beverly D.	HM1
RAWSON, Arthur D.	DCW2
REBER, Lewis J.	HMC
REED, Richard C.	HM3
REED, William T.	HM1
RICE, George (n)	HMC
RICHARDS, Morris C.	HM2
RICHARDSON, Howard D.	HN
RICHIE, Oscar (n)	HN
RICHMOND, Sindney L.	HM2
ROBINSON, Ralph W.	HM1
RODRIGUEZ, Jose E.	HM1
ROETTGER, Frederick C.	HM2
ROHLER, Eddie A., Jr.	HM3
ROST, John E.	HM3
ROSE, Vincent L.	HM1
ROTH, Clarence J.	HM2
ROUDEBUSH, Alvin (n)	HM1
ROWLETT, Lonnie (n)	HM1
RUBLE, Estern H.	HM2
RUELIUS, Thomas L.	HM3
RULON, Wayne L.	HMC
RUSSELL, Manly O.	EMPFN
RUTH, Wilbur M.	HM2
SALISBURY, E. E.	CSR1
SAUNDERS, John W.	HM2
SCHAEFFER, Merle J.	HN
SCHERLER, Jacque W.	HM3
SCHMIT, Richard W.	HM3
SCOTT, Stanley E.	HM2
SEARS, Jay D.	HM1
SEMERAD, Albert J.	HM3
SESTO, Joseph J.	HM1

Rate	Name		Rate	Name
IIM3	WILLIAMS, Victor H.		HM	C. W. F. CHILDRESS
HMC	WILSON, William D.		HM	A. HALL
HN	WINANS, Morel (n)		HM	J. T. WADE
HMC	WISHART, Bruce B.		HM	E. F. POWER
HM3	WOLFE, Guy E.		HM	C. M. MC CURDY
HMC	WOOD, Merle E.		HM	K. LOU
HM1	WOOD, Willis J.		HM	C. R. SCHNELLE
HM2	WOOD, Wright W.		HM	W. R. NEVINS
HN	WOODS, Gerald P.		HM	L. R. SMITH
HMC	WOOTEN, Carl E.		HM	C. TRNCHTENBARG
HM2	WRIGHT, Clyde L.		HM	B. ROTHCHILD
HM3	WYATT, Edwin L.		HM	F. W. DISCHINGER
HM2	WYMAN, James T.		HM	A. J. MC FARLIN
HM3	XANDER, Gene O.		HM	J. T. COY
CSG1	ZARETZKY, Paul E.		HM	D. J. RHODES
HM3	ZNIDAR, Stanley A.		HM	R. H. BROWN
HM3	J. L. MORRIS		HM	C. M. CARTER
HMC	J. H. JOHNSON		HM	E. M. GRIJALVA
HMC	H. D. CANFIELD		HM	J. S. BROWNING
HM1	R. F. DENGLAS		HM	J. B. SAILEE
HM2	J. W. HOLLAND		HM	D. E. WALKER
HM3	S. C. WATKINS		HM	S. WILLIAMS
HM1	J. F. NORMAN		HN	R. WILLIAMS
HM3	F. C. SHEA			D. C. DUTT
HM1	E. E. SILVER, JR.			N. D. REED
HM1	C. H. PATTS			D. COMSTOCK
HM2	H. W. COURSEY			J. L. WALKER
HM3	T. C. HASTINGS			R. J. CRERAR
IIMC	M. BRODNAX			B. BROODER
HM1	R. B. BABBITT			V. B. EWING
HM1	W. M. BYERS			E. L. STORMS
HM2	G. E. DEVAUL			R. E. CRUMBLESS
HM3	F. H. GIFFORD			A. S. LEWIS
HM2	R. L. GOSNEL			D. H. COOK
IIM2	R. W. LYSTRA			W. T. BANKS
HMC	L. T. EDWARDS			F. GARDEA
HM1	G. S. SMI.			F. E. BALENTINE
HM1	C. SVOBDA			J. W. HAINES
HM1	J. E. ROBER.			J. L. STRIDER
HM1	W. F. ALLEN			

Rate	Name		Rate	Name
HM1	SEYLER, Richard J.		HM3	TENCH, Elwood R.
HM3	RHEALEY, Clyne R.		HM3	THOMAS, Claude R.
HMC	SHONK, Orvel T., Jr.		HM2	THOMAS, Gordon M.
HM3	SIMON, Arthur L.		IIN	THOMSEN, Alfred W.
HM3	SKIBA, George J.		EM1	TIMMERMAN, Alan N.
HM2	SLATTERY, Louis L.		HN	TINSLEY, Thomas S.
HMC	SMITH, Bill J.		IIM3	TITTLE, Albert C.
HMC	SMITH, Darryl W.		SN	TKACH, Paul M.
HMC	SMITH, George A.		CSG1	●TOUSSAINT, William F.
HN	SMITH, Harry H.		HN	TRUDELL, John J.
HM3	SMITH, Hugh A.		HM2	TRUDELL, Donald J.
IIN	SMITH, John O.		IIN	TURK, Joe P.
HM3	SMITH, Nathan T., Jr.		IIM3	TURPAK, Robert P.
HM3	SMITH, Richard (n) Jr.		HM1	UNVER, "J" "H"
HM3	SMITH, Richard J.		IIM3	VAN CLEAVE, Kenneth W.
HM1	SMITH, Robert K.		IIM3	VAN WAGONER, Alvah J.
HN	SPENCER, Robert D.		HM3	VAN WIE, Earl B.
SN	STACEY, Charles G.		IIM3	VASERBERG, Ralph (n)
HM2	STALLINGS, Thomas D.		HMC	VAUGHN, Lee M.
HM2	STANLEY, Ralph V.		HMC	VAUGHN, Lew H.
HM2	STANTURF, Richard W.		IIN	VIZINET, Jnmy (n)
IIN	STEIN, Wallace M.		HMC	WALKER, Charles R.
HM3	STEPHENSON, Billy C.		IIM3	WALSH, James F.
HM1	STERIS, Leonard (n)		FN	WARR, George (n)
HM3	STEWART, John D.		IIM3	WATSON, Donald (n) Jr.
HN	STOKER, William A., Jr.		IIM3	WENTWORTH, Eugene F.
HM1	STONE, Elmo R.		HM2	WENTWORTH, Richard L.
HN	STORMS, Daniel E.		CSG1	WEST, Roy F.
HM3	STORY, Leonard M.		IIM3	WEYANT, Cornelius M.
IIN	STRONG, Jack B., Jr.		EMP2	WHITE, Donald L.
HMC	STURTEVANT, Silas V.		MER3	WHITE, Leland T.
HN	SUDDUTH, Marvin T.		HN	WHITE, Stanley E.
IIM3	SULLINS, Jesse O., Jr.		IIM1	WICHMAN, George H.
HM2	TANNER, Arthur P.		IIN	WIESE, William D.
SN	TAYLOR, Donald O.		IIM3	WILES, Earl F.
HM1	TAYLOR, Eugene M.		IIM1	WILKERSON, John H.
IIM3	TAYLOR, John R.		IIM3	WILKINSON, Otis E.
HN	TEEL, Robert W.		IIM1	WILLIAMS, James O.

COMMISSARY PERSONNEL

W. H. BASSETT
SIONED WARRANT OFFICER HC
COMMISSARY OFFICER

M. O'NEILL
LIEUTENANT, NC, U. S. NAVY
DIETITIAN

B. SMITH
LIEUTENANT, NC, U. S. NAVY
ASSISTANT DIETITIAN

H. A. OAKES HMC, B. B. WISHART HMC, A. W. MOSS
CHIEF COMMISSARY STEWARDS

	O ICE ER L		
HN	T HM1	A. H. PLA	I
	P. NEIDLING HM1		
STEP			
STER	WARD SERVICE		
STEW VAK	HM1	D. A. LYONS	HM1
STO WILLIAMS	HM1	A. C. MC MILLEN	HM1
C. HIGGINS	HM3	W. R BATTS	HM3

MAIN MESS HALL.

R. ROWLAND	ME2	S. L. BALLA	HM3

MAIN KITCHEN

SAINT	CSG1	F. M. JOHNSON	SR1
	CSG1	P. E. ZAR T	H
TAY SBURY	CSR1	W. J. C SON, John	
TA E	CSG2	W. INSON, Od	3
MO ROW	CSG3	LIAMS, Ja	

Appendix 5
Tea With President and Mrs. Truman

In 1952 during the Korean War, the White House was being renovated. During that period the President, Mrs. Truman and Margaret were living in Blair house. Many of the young marines returned from that war with frost bite, due to the harsh winter weather in Korea. Many of these young men were forced to undergo amputations. The President and Mrs. Truman invited these young men to Tea with them. It was requested to have a Navy nurse accompany them to Blair House for the Tea. I volunteered to be the nurse to accompany the men in the photo. Navy pictures were taken to mark the occasion on this brisk day in 1952. Accompanying this article is a photo of the described occasion.

Submitted by: Joan H. Weber (formerly LT. (j.g.) Joan Hancock)
             Stationed at Bethesda Naval Hospital 1952
             Bethesda, Md.

Appendix 6

Charge Nurse's Schedule

Navy Nurse Commander Lura Jane Emery, Nurse Corps, US Navy (Ret) provided the following which describes a charge nurse's duty aboard a hospital ship in a combat area. Emery served aboard the USS REPOSE (AH-16) during the Korean War.

0530 *All blood and urine samples are collected and sent to the lab.*

0700 *The day nurse reporting for duty receives reports from the night nursing supervisor and night corpsmen. These reports cover everything that has transpired during the night involving the patients like new admissions, orders (instructions from the doctors), surgery, vital signs if elevated and the administering of pain medications.*

0715 *Ensure that all patients get breakfast and the blind are fed. Record intake and output on patients as ordered by the doctor.*

    Make out corpsman detail as to what patients each corpsman will care for. He is responsible for bathing the patient, attending to his personal hygiene (teeth brushing) and change the linen on his bed.

    Medication Corpsman: Prepare and distributes medications at 0700 and 0800. Records all medications given throughout the day. Nurses are the only one who are authorized to distribute narcotic medications. These are kept under lock and key by the ward nurse.

    Dressing Corpsman: Redresses all wounded as ordered by the doctor. Re-sterilizes instruments on the dressing cart like forceps and re-supplies dressing cart. Charts all changes along with appearance of the wound i.e. drainage of the wound.

    Cast Room Corpsman: Cuts off or applies casts to patients as ordered by the doctor.

0800 *Ready for A.M. Sick Call.*
    Have vital signs log ready for the doctor to note temperature, pulse, respiration and blood pressure. Accompany the doctor on his rounds and informing him of any changes or unusual symptoms for each patient. Have all lab and x-ray reports available. Records doctor's orders and have him sign the report.

    As soon as Sick Call is over, the nurse updates each chart to add or delete certain medications and to include orders such as x-rays and lab tests. Orders for the later are written up and submitted to the appropriate departments. Ensure that patients full fill requirements such as going to physical therapy.

    Prepare charts for patients leaving the ship for the continental US.

Administer all pre-op medications to patients going to surgery. Care for post-op patients. Check their orders and carry out orders as required like connecting indwelling catheters to a bag.

Post-op patients with chest tubes must be connected to a special vacuum. Patients with a card [?] must have their circulation checked frequently. All post op patients must have vital signs taken every 15 minutes for several hours to watch for shock/and or hemorrhages.

1130   *Serve chow. Check to see if patients are eating and drinking fluids. Chart intake and output.*

1300   *Rest hour from 1300-1400 (1 p.m. until 2 p.m.). Darken ward. Keep ward quiet.*

1400-1600   *Check vital signs as ordered. Admit and discharge patients. Our patients usually arrived by train at the depot next to the ship between midnight and 0630. So we were used as a base facility to admit and get patients ready for transfer to the continental US. Patients usually went to surgery to have shrapnel removed shortly after they arrived aboard ship. After 24-48 hours, patients were moved out to make room for new admissions.*

1600-0700   *The same routine continued – its called 'caring for patients'. Most patients had special needs or requirements. You kept the sickest patients close to the nursing station for constant observation. Most patients slept a great deal after their surgery.*

As nurses we had a brief period of quiet during our dinnertime and for about one hour after that. I used this time to shower and put on clean clothes.

What Emery described became amplified a hundred times over as Naval Hospital Yokosuka and the three hospital ships, CONSOLATION, REPOSE and HAVEN were bombarded by an intense, overwhelming patient load. The Navy nurse of the Korean War were not just ordinary women complying with what the Navy Nurses Guide describes as a sterile medical environment.

Appendix 7
Colombian Soldier's Letter

Korea
Oct. 31, 1951

"Señorita Haire:"
((author's translator's note: This soldier has
a great deal of admiration and respect for you);
It has been difficult for me to translate his
friendly attitude, and deep appreciation with
the colour an vehemence expressed in his
original letter written in his own tongue). There-
fore, with an understanding of his people,
I have attempted to interpret the friendship
he feels for you). On a subsequent sheet of paper
I have translated the Poetical "Allegiance
of a Columbian Soldier, which he thought you
might like. This he does to impress you as
he would one of his own country women; viz.
The pride of a fighting man)).

"The enclosed, my allegiance to my country,
which to you has but little significance (merit),
but means a great deal to me and every
Columbian soldier fighting to protect his
country and keep it free — a democracy!
My offer is small, "the allegiance
of a Columbian Soldier", one wounded
in combat, in a distant land, who has
been fortunately blessed to have been
care for by you and your assistants on
board the U. S. S. Consolation.

II

this, a memoir, which I shall always
treasure — Of a grateful Columbian
soldier cared for by a beautiful, American
nurse, who was attentive and kind;
who sought cheer, comfort, and understand, unbiasedly, all whom she cared
for.

My heart is filled with sadness
for I have not been able to express,
personally, my appreciation. Although
we may seem to be worlds apart as
regards our languages, I'm sure
you will understand. "a glance
of appreciation" is a universal sign.

When, with the help of God, I
regress to my country, your kindness and
understanding, qualities which have
increased your beauty a thousand fold,
shall be made known to my
compatriots.

I leave, a soldier, to return to
the battle fronts, a full heart and,
                    Your servant

A Columbian Soldier's Allegiance
To His Country.
Columbia – my Country – Thy Banners
I hold dear to my heart.
I believe in your destiny.
I wish to see you forever free –
great and respected.
Thy glories, thy beauty – my home.
'In thee I see my ambitions bloom
The tombs of thy heroes – monuments
To freedom true –
Like them, I shall dedicate my
life, my strength toward your freedom –
The realization of my dreams.
To be your protector – My glory!

Courtesy of Marion Haire

Appendix 8
Letter from the War Zone

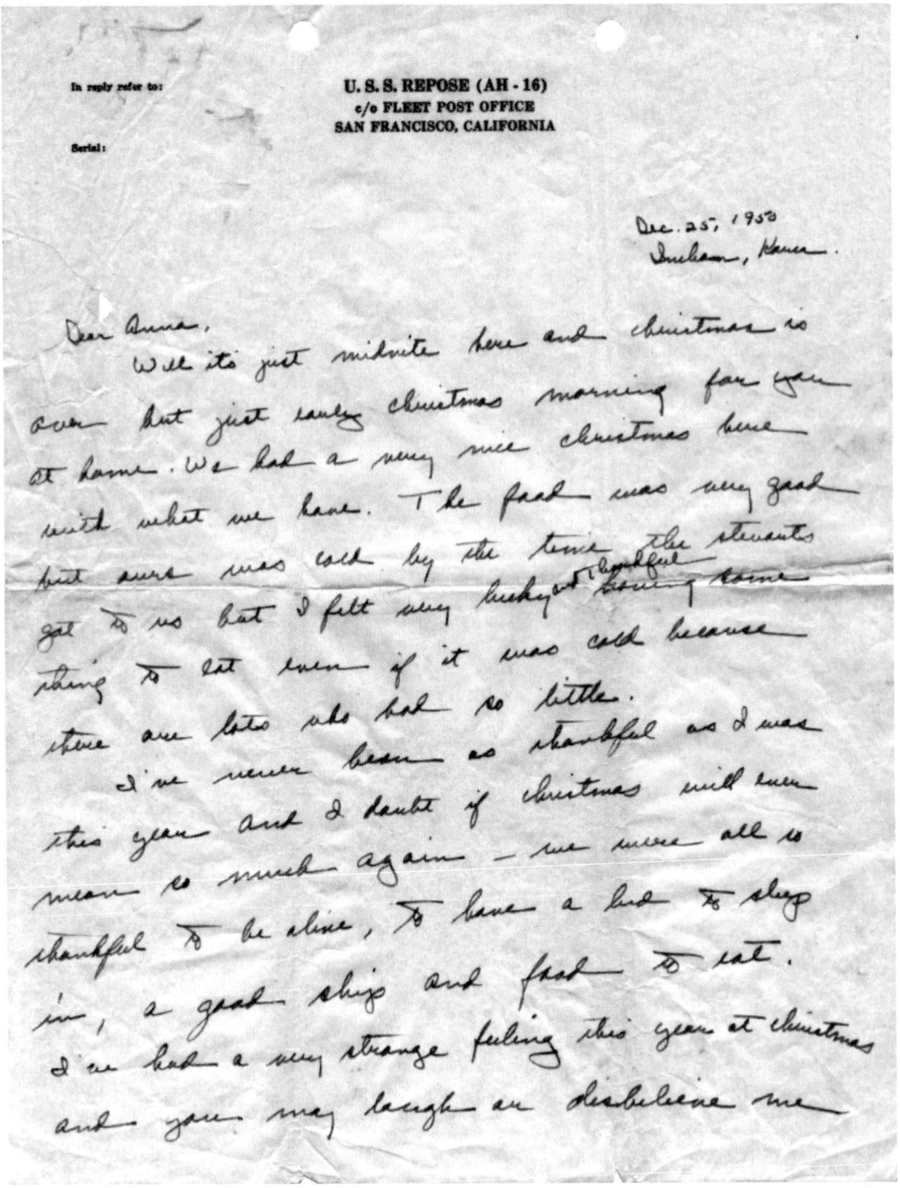

In reply refer to:

Serial:

U. S. S. REPOSE (AH - 16)
c/o FLEET POST OFFICE
SAN FRANCISCO, CALIFORNIA

Dec. 25, 1950
Inchon, Korea.

Dear Anna,

Well its just midnite here and christmas is over but just early christmas morning for you at home. We had a very nice christmas here with what we have. The food was very good but sure was cold by the time the stewards got to us but I felt very lucky and thankful having some thing to eat even if it was cold because there are lots who had so little.

I've never been as thankful as I was this year and I doubt if christmas will ever mean so much again — we were all so thankful to be alive, to have a bed to sleep in, a good ship and food to eat. I've had a very strange feeling this year at christmas and you may laugh or disbelieve me

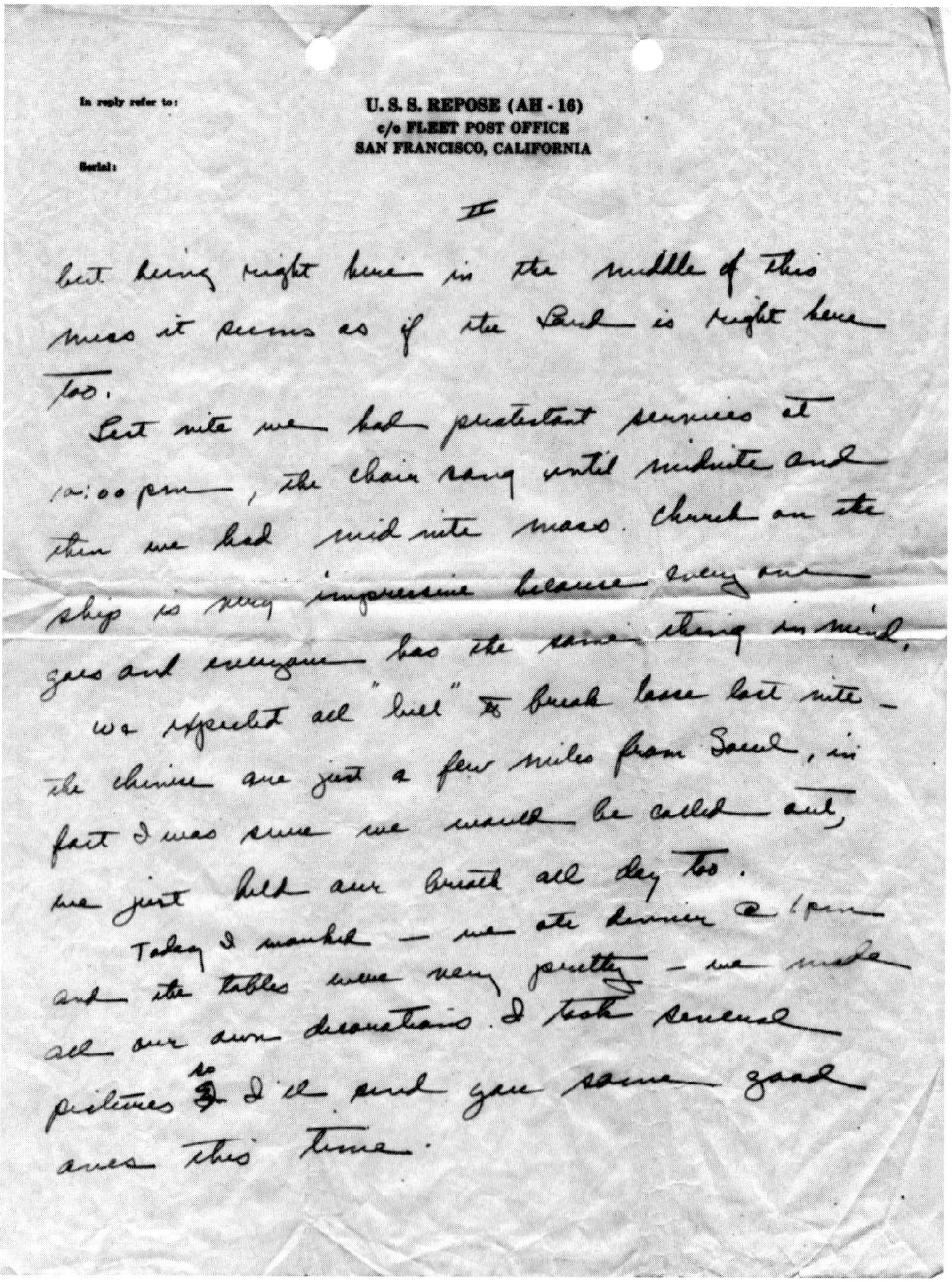

In reply refer to:

U. S. S. REPOSE (AH - 16)
c/o FLEET POST OFFICE
SAN FRANCISCO, CALIFORNIA

Serial:

II

but being right here in the middle of this
mess it seems as if the Devil is right here
too.

Last nite we had protestant services at
10:00 pm, the choir sang until midnite and
then we had mid nite mass. church on the
ship is very impressive because every one
goes and everyone has the same thing in mind.
We expected all "hell" to break loose last nite —
the chinese are just a few miles from Seoul, in
fact I was sure we would be called out,
we just held our breath all day too.

Today I worked — we ate dinner @ 1 pm
and the tables were very pretty — we made
all our own decorations. I took several
pictures too I'll send you some good
ones this time.

U. S. S. REPOSE (AH - 16)
c/o FLEET POST OFFICE
SAN FRANCISCO, CALIFORNIA

In reply refer to:

Serial:

I am trying to get several good ones so I can have one enlarged to send home.

This p.m. we had a party — all of us pulled names and gave these real simple things. I got a can of tobacco to roll my own cigarettes. Some made simple dolls and all sorts of things. They gave the chaplain a pair of huge shorts ē Ants painted on the back in red ink and they had a real cute poem in about going to see the Bishop in the shorts.

The cookies haven't arrived yet and I haven't gotten my permanent. I only got about three Christmas cards, I guess our mail is being held in Japan.

It's late and I must get up in the A.M. so must close — give my best to all and take care of yourself.

Love.
Jane

Notes

1. Navy Nurses Guide, OA, NHC.

2. Op. Cit.

3. Author interview with Virginia Jennings Watson, NC, USN

4. Op. cit. p.22

5. Op. cit.

6. Author interview with Marilyn Ewing Affleck, NC, USN

7. Annual Report, Navy Military Personnel Statistics (NAVPERS 15659(A), 30 June 1973, OA, NHC.

8. Capt. Doris M. Sterner, NC, USN (Ret.), *In and Out of Harms Way.*

9. Historical Narrative, serial NH3923:17:NBC:IV A12, 1 March 1951, OA, NHC.

10. This quote is a composite of comments from several persons interviewed.

11. Historical Narrative, Commander Fleet Activities, Yokosuka, Japan, 1 July 1949 to 31 December 1949, OA, NHC.

12. Tom Tompkins, *Yokosuka: Base of an Empire.*

13. Op. cit.

14. History of the Yokosuka Naval Base, Chronological File, Yokosuka Fleet Activities, OA, NHC.

15. Tompkins. Op. cit.

16. Operational Archives Record of the Naval Nurse Corps. Box 12, folder #1.

17. Op. cit.

18. Op. cit.

19. Op. cit.

20. Op. cit.

21. Lt. Comdr. Alberts Burk, NC,USN, letter to Capt. Winnie Gibson, NC, USN, 13 April 1951, Record of the Naval Nurse Corps, Box 12, Folder #1, OA.

22. Ibid.

23. Op. cit.

24. Op. cit.

25. All above quoted information came also from Box 12. See footnote 21.

26. *U. S. Armed Forces Medical Journal*, Navy Bureau of Medicine Archives, Vol III, #1, p. 95-103.

27. Op. cit.

28. Author interview, Comdr. Lura Jane Emery, NC, USN (Ret).

29. Tom Tompkins, Ibid.

30. Op. cit. p. 37.

31. Operational Archives Naval Historical Center, Chronological file, Yokosuka.

32. L. Kraeer Ferguson and Lillian A. Sholtis. *Eliason's Surgical Nursing.* (J.B. Lippencott Co, Phila. 1959) p. 621.

33. OANHC, box 12.

34. OANHC, box 12

35. This information given to me by Virginia Jennings Watson was taken from a magazine article dating back to the 1950s, magazine name unknown, article: "The world's most surprising mountain," by Wm. L. Worden.

36. This information taken from the "War Diary," *Consolation,* reprinted from the 1953 Cruise Book, Navy Bureau of Medicine & Surgery Archives (NBMSA)

37. Op. cit.

38. *Consolation* War Diary, Operational Archives National Historical Center. OANHC

39. Op. cit.

40. Op. cit.

41. *All Hands Magazine,* April 1951, MBMSA

42. Cruise Book NBMSA.

43. Op. cit.

44. *Leatherneck,* September, 1952. NBMSA.

45. *Consolation* 1953 Cruise Book, NBMSA.

46. In folder *"Repose,"* "History USS *Repose"* NBMSA.

47. From folder *"Repose,"* NBMSA, report "A Review of Two Years Operations of the USS *Repose,* AH-16, in the Korean Theater of Operations, 20 September 1950- 20 September 1952."

48. Ibid.

49. Ibid.

50. *Repose* folder, Cruise book for 1952. NBMSA

51. "The Ship With a Heart," *Life and Health Magazine, July* 1952, NBMSA

52. *Life and Health magazine,* July 1952, p. 32)

53. A Review of Two Years Operation of the USS *Repose* (AH-16) In the Korean Theater of Operations from 20 September 1950 to 20 September 1952. NBMSA

54. "Hospital Ship Rescues GIs With Inches to Spare," *The Evening Star,* December 1950. NBMS A

55. According to the report "A Review of Two Years of Operations, etc." OP, CIT.

56. From a partial newspaper article, ". . . Laudatory letters from Commanders," found in the *Repose* folder NBMSA

57. From *Repose two-year report. NBMSA*

58. *Repose* Cruise book, 1953. NBMSA

59. Eleanor Harrington, "Aboard a Hospital Ship," *The American Journal of Nursing,* May 1953, Vol. 53, #5, NBMSA

60. History of USS *Haven* (AH-12), serial AH12/16 5750, 15 July 1959, Command Files, USS *Haven* OA NHC.

61. Harrington. Op. cit.

62. *Haven,* War Diary, 15 September 1950 to 28 February 1951, OA NHC

63. Harrington, Op. cit.

64. Record of Naval Nurse Corps. Box 12. Op. cit.

65. Operational Archives, Navy Historical Center

66. Harrington. Op. cit. NBMSA

67. Maryann Callan, "Lack of Aid, Blood for Wounded Told, Conditions Found on US Hospital Ship. Off Korea, related by Angeleno." *LA Times NBMSA*

68. *Purple Heart Magazine,* Sept-Oct 1995, p. 28.

Bibliography

Ebbert, Jean and Marie-Beth Hall. *Crossed Currents: Navy Women from WWI to Tailhook*. Washington, DC: Brassey's Inc., 1993.

Fehrenbach, T.R. *This Kind of War: The Classic Korean War History, Second edition*. Washington DC: Brassey's, 1998.

Ferguson, L. Kraeer and Lillian A. Sholtis. *Eliason's Surgical Nursing*. Philadelphia: J.B. Lippincott Company, 1959.

Forty, George. *At War in Korea*. London: Arms and Armour Press, 1997. (First published 1982 by Ian Allan Ltd.)

Hammel, Eric M. *Chosin: A Heroic Ordeal of the Korean War*. New York: The Vanguard Press, 1981.

Hastings, Max. *The Korean War*. New York: Simon and Schuster, 1987.

Highsmith, Carol M. and Ted Landphair. *Forgotten No More: The Korean War Veterans Memorial Story*. Washington DC: Chelsea Publishing, Inc., 1995.

Holm, Jeanne, Maj Gen, USAF (Ret). *Women in the Military: An Unfinished Revolution*. Novato, CA: Presidio Press, 1992.

Kaufman, Burton I. *The Korean Conflict*. Westport, CN: Greenwood Press. 1999.

Knox, Donald. *The Korean War: Pusan to Chosin, An Oral History*. New York: Harcourt, Brace, Jovanovich Publishers, 1985.

Murphy, Edward F. *Korean War Heroes*. Novato, CA: Presidio Press, 1992.

Owen, Joseph R. *Colder than Hell: A Marine Rifle Company at Chosin Reservoir*. New York: Ivy Books/Ballantine, 1996.

Pratt, Sherman, LTC, USA (Ret). *Decisive Battles of the Korean War: An Infantry Company Commander's View of the War's Most Critical Engagements*. New York: Vantage Press, 1992.

Russ, Martin. *Breakout: The Chosin Reservoir Campaign, Korean 1950*. New York: Fromm International, 1999.

Sterner, Doris M., Captain, Nurse Corps, USN (Ret). *In and Out of Harms Way: A History of the Navy Nurse Corps*. Seattle: Peanut Butter Publishing, 1996.

Stokesbury, James L. *A Short History of the Korean War*. New York: W, Morrow and Co., 1988.

Summers, Harry, Jr. *Korean War Almanac*. New York: Facts on File, Inc., 1990.

Tompkins, Tom. *Yokosuka: Base of an Empire*. Novato, CA: Presidio Press, 1981.

Websites:

http://korea50.army.mil

http://nnca.org

http://www.lonesailor.org

http://oldbreed@aol.com

http://www.mca-marine.org

http://www.history.navy.mil

http://www.nps.gov

http://www.womensmemorial.org

http://www.inc.com

http://www.va/womenvet

http://www.userpages.aug.com

Index

Note: Page numbers in **bold** *indicate photographs and illustrations.*

ORDER FORM

NAME _____

ADDRESS _____

CITY/STATE _____ ZIP/POSTAL CODE _____

PHONE _____ COUNTRY (OUTSIDE U.S.A.) _____

TITLE	QTY	PRICE	TOTAL
QUIET HEROES		$18.95	. . . .

SHIPPING:
US orders shipped by Priority Mail.
Canadian orders shipped by Air Mail.
First book: $4.50 ($6.60 in Canada).
Each additional book: $2.00 ($3.00 in Canada).
For UPS rates, bulk disount orders, or
foreign rates, call us at 651-490-9408.

TOTAL _____
MN residents add sales tax _____
Shipping _____
TOTAL ENCLOSED _____
(US Funds only)

❏ Check   ❏ Money order   ❏ Visa   ❏ M/C   ❏ Discover   ❏ AMEX

Card #_____ Exp. date_____

Signature_____

4 Ways to Order

Mail: 2700 Rice St. • St. Paul, MN 55113
(check or credit card)

Toll-Free Phone: 1-888-220-5402
(9 am–5 pm CT Monday – Friday, US/Canada only)

FAX: 1-651-490-1450

E-Mail: SmitHseprs@aol.com

Smith House Press